TEAM RACING *for* SAILBOATS

Second Edition

Worlds 1995 – The author and Mel Hughes

TEAM RACING *for* SAILBOATS

Steve Tylecote

Second Edition

with a
Foreword
by
John Reed
of
The Eric Twiname Memorial Trust

FOREWORD

The Eric Twiname Memorial Trust is delighted to sponsor the publication of this important new sailing book, now in its second edition, at this appropriate time. Team Racing, having dropped out of the popular sailing endeavours over the past two decades, is experiencing a most healthy revival, probably initiated by the establishment of the World Team Racing Championship by the International Sailing Federation. It is largely the sailing activity of the young – school and university sailors – the principal area in which the Trust operates, and it was the great speciality of the late Eric Twiname.

Those of us who knew Eric will find it hard to believe that he died in 1979 and it comes as a shock to realise that many sailing today were not even born then. So, asking forgiveness from those who are of a more mature generation we will answer the question – Who was Eric Twiname?

He was a rare individual who could excel at many things. He was a brilliant pianist, a prolific writer of books, articles and plays and a superb sailor. Taught at an early age by his father it was in this activity that Eric really excelled and, in addition to winning many championships in GP14s, Lasers and International Canoes, he had a profound influence on the administration of sailing, both in the area of the Racing Rules (his book, **The Rules Book** (1977), was a sailing best-seller) and in writing what was, for many years, the definitive book on the subject, **Dinghy Team Racing**, published in 1971 and now long out-of-print – and this is where we came in.

The Trust was set up in an informal way in 1980 by his father Alec in order to continue Eric's many and diverse interests in sailing. At first the Trust responded to calls for funding from many areas, including round the world yachtsmen, disabled sailors and Olympic campaigns, Alec paying the grants out of his own pocket. However a more formal approach emerged with the formation as a Charitable Trust, with a concentration on youth sailing, especially racing. Alec Twiname settled an amount of capital on the Trust which was invested to provide a steady annual income.

Alec died in 1996 and the Trust is now headed by his widow, Hazel. The finances of the Trust and the designation of funds are run by a small team of Trustees, all sailors who knew Eric well. The administration is run on a voluntary basis, so overheads are minimal and the revenue – consisting of fundraising, small donations and the income of capital – is always put to optimum effect. There cannot be many young sailors who have not been helped in some way by the Trust, be it through the provision of support and coaching boats to all Youth classes, the grants given to Optimist courses or the financing of BUSA administration.

The sponsorship of this book is a new initiative and we hope that it will be of great value to those involved in, or taking up, team racing.

John Reed
The Administrator
The Eric Twiname Memorial Trust
Bordon, Hampshire, UK

The photograph opposite shows a Firefly dinghy, extensively used in team racing, presented to the Hamble River Youth Initiative by the Eric Twiname Trust

Copyright © 2002 Fernhurst Books

First published in 2002 by:
Fernhurst Books,
Duke's Path, High Street,
Arundel, West Sussex,
BN18 9AJ, UK
Tel: 01903 882277   email: sales@fernhurstbooks.co.uk
Fax: 01903 882715   web: www.fernhurstbooks.co.uk

The first edition was published by Fernhurst Books in 1999

British Library Cataloguing in Publication Data:
A catalogue record for this book is available from the British Library

ISBN **1 898660 85 9**

Printed and bound in China through **World Print**

The author thanks the following for their help with the efforts for the first edition:
Martin Smethers, Nick Ross, Greg Ansell, Chris Atkins, Peter Waine, Bruce Hebbert, Melanie Hughes, Tiggy Ansell, Damian Boreham, Geoff Jackson, Fiona Coates, Ricky Tagg, Greg Eaton, Roger Morris, Stuart Hudson, David Ellis, Gilly Ansell and Colin Gordon
Particular thanks for help with the Second Edition are due to Greg Ansell, Tiggy Ansell, Hugh Wylan, Fiona Coates and Parry Coates. In addition particular thanks for advice on contemporary rule application from Chris Atkins, Nick Ross and John Doerr

The author is particularly grateful to Tiggy Ansell for all the photographs reproduced in the book

Design, illustrations, typesetting and editing by **John Carden**

Cover design by **Simon Balley**

Set in 9/11pt Eras Book

CONTENTS

1.6.2.5 Tacking out 35
1.6.2.6 Penalty turns 36
1.6.2.7 Sailing the groove 37
1.6.2.8 Individual starting skills 37
1.6.3 Dealing with the Rules 37
1.6.3.1 Understanding the
         structure of the Rules 37
1.6.3.2 The incident process 38
1.6.3.3 Transitions 39
1.6.3.4 Racing when umpired 40

Part II
Team Racing Manoeuvres 45
Chapter 2 – Pre-Start Manoeuvres 47
2.1 Basic Pre-Start 47
2.1.1 Controlling and escaping 47
2.1.2 Heading right 48
2.1.3 Heading left 48
2.2 Advanced Pre-Start 50
2.2.1 Tailing in, forcing high 51
2.2.2 Leading in, killing time 52
2.2.3 Force out at either end 54
2.2.4 Establishing pre-start overlaps 54

Chapter 3 – Team Starting Manoeuvres 55
3.1 Basic Starting 55
3.1.1 Time traps 55
3.1.2 Being in a particular place
       on the line – location logic 55
3.1.2.1 Winning the ends 56
3.1.3 Bad starts – the great escapes 58
3.2 Advanced Starting 59
3.2.1 Team geographic start 59
3.2.2 Match race starts 60

Chapter 4 – Upwind Manoeuvres 61
4.1 Basic Upwind Manoeuvres 61
4.1.1 The Squeeze 61
4.1.2 Covering 61
4.1.2.1 The close cover 61
4.1.2.2 Tack out and prevention 62
4.1.3 Tacking duel 62
4.1.4 Remote or loose cover 63
4.1.5 Lee bow tack 64
4.1.6 Using obstructions 66
4.2 Advanced Upwind Manoeuvres 68
4.2.1 Gybe out of a close cover 68
4.2.2 Dummy tack 70
4.2.3 Double tack 71
4.2.4 Managing the pairs – team covering 71
4.2.5 Swap cover and cannot tack 72
4.2.6 The close cover tack/
       the close duck –
       Slam Dunk of old 75

Part I
Team Racing – The Basics 9
Chapter 1 – Team Racing Knowledge 10
1.1 Characteristics of Team Racing 10
1.2 Types of team racing 10
1.2.1 Two-boat racing 10
1.2.2 Three-boat racing 11
1.2.3 Four-boat racing 11
1.2.4 Why team race? 11
1.3 Types of Event 11
1.4 Strategy – Skill – Manoeuvre 12
1.5 Basic strategic concepts 12
1.5.1 Examine the Event Format 12
1.5.2 Assess the Sailing Area 12
1.5.3 Assess you team's strengths
       & weaknesses 14
1.5.4 Assess the opposition 14
1.5.5 Assess the opposition's
       expected strategy 14
1.6 Skills 14
1.6.1 Tactical considerations 14
1.6.1.1 Winning or losing? 14
1.6.1.2 Stable or unstable? 14
1.6.1.3 Team or Fleet 17
1.6.1.4 Focus 17
1.6.1.5 Mind the Gap –
         The Push-Pull Effect 19
1.6.1.6 Time – the other dimension 20
1.6.1.7 Balance and leverage 20
1.6.1.8 Attack and control from astern 21
1.6.1.9 Preparing your strategy 23
1.6.1.10 Three boat racing combinations 23
1.6.1.11 Summary of key tactical features 29
1.6.1.12 Tactical Commandments:
         Do's & Don'ts 30
1.6.2 Boat positioning skills 30
1.6.2.1 Windshadow control 31
1.6.2.2 How to slow down 32
1.6.2.3 Boat positioning –
         the control zone 32
1.6.2.4 The Lee Bow Position 34

Chapter 5 – Reaching Manoeuvres 77
5.1 Reaching Manoeuvres 77
     5.1.1   Room? 77
     5.1.2   Reaching: leading boat attacks to
             windward 77
     5.1.3   Slow and trap to leeward 79
     5.1.4   Working together – the "High–Low" 79
     5.1.5   Breaking the overlap 82
     5.1.6   The stages of the reach 83
             5.1.6.1 Tactical considerations 83

Chapter 6 – Running Manoeuvres 85
6.1 Basic Running Manoeuvres 85
     6.1.1   Keeping a lead 85
     6.1.2   The Flier – sailing off to one
             side of the run 85
     6.1.3   Running overlaps 86
6.2 Advanced Running Manoeuvres 86
     6.2.1   Close cover 86
     6.2.2   Close cover – the gybing duel 87
     6.2.3   Trap to starboard from astern 88
     6.2.4   The port luff 88
     6.2.5   Double gybe and luff 89
     6.2.6   Breaking the overlap 90
     6.2.7   Sailing beyond the layline 91
     6.2.8   The tack out 92
     6.2.9   The asymmetric trap 93

Chapter 7 – Mark Rounding Manoeuvres 94
7.1 Key Mark Rounding Objectives 94
     7.1.1   Mark 'Rules' 94
7.2 Basic Mark Manoeuvres 99
     7.2.1   Stopping in the two length zone 99
     7.2.2   The sail past the mark 100
     7.2.3   The tempting gap 101
7.3 Advanced Mark Rounding Manoeuvres 101
     7.3.1   Upwind mark rounding – key
             differences from downwind marks 101
     7.3.2   Windward mark – boats on
             opposite tacks 103
     7.3.3   Windward marks – stopping boat
             will not need to tack 105
     7.3.4   Leeward mark to port 107

7.3.5   Leeward mark to starboard 109
7.3.6   Stopping at the finish 109

Part III
The Winning Team 111
Chapter 8 – The Winning Team 113
8.1 Team Preparation 113
     8.1.1   Team basics 113
     8.1.2   Team dynamics 113
     8.1.3   Winning the battle of the minds 113
     8.1.4   Selection 114
     8.1.5   Coaching and leadership 115
     8.1.6   Practice options 115
8.2 The Team Racing Rules Appendix
     (ISAF Rules Appendix D) – An Explanation 117
     8.2.1   The changes to the Rules 117
     8.2.2   Modifications to Protests and Incident
             Management when team racing 118
     8.2.3   Modifications to scoring while
             team racing 119
     8.2.4   Other modifications to look for 119
     8.2.5   The relevance of the
             Sailing Instructions 119
8.3 The Winning Strategy 120
     8.3.1   Risk based decisions 120
     8.3.2   Managing the combinations 121
     8.3.3   Managing 4-boat team
             racing combinations 121
8.4 Umpires and Incidents 122
     8.4.1   Tips for team race umpires 122
8.5 Team Race Crewing 122
     8.5.1   Crew boat handling 123
     8.5.2   Crew race handling 123
     8.5.3   Crew–Helm psychology 123
     8.5.4   Minimum weight limit 123
8.6 Team Racing for Kids 123
     8.6.1   Keep it simple 124
     8.6.2   Safety 124
     8.6.3   Kids & the coach's mind-set 124
8.7 What It's All About... (Really) 125
8.8 Bringing It All Together 125

Sources of Information & Useful Addresses 126

PART I
TEAM RACING: THE BASICS

Part I of this book is designed to give you a background to team racing. It introduces you to the key **fundamentals**, which are shared by event organisers and competitors. It explains the differences which occur when there are **two, three or four boats** in a team.

Basic **strategic concepts** are explained and the **'language'** of team racing is made clear by defining many of the important terms which are used to describe tactics and racing situations.

Part I then moves on to look at how race tactics are influenced by the team **'combination'** of positions. This gives you a guide as to what you should be trying to achieve when you are racing.

Part I then concludes with a detailed look at the **key skills** required to team race effectively. In doing this many important race situations are explained. The way the **racing rules** are designed to work, and how they apply to an **'incident'** are also covered so you can be confident when **using the rules**.

Part I is all about Team Racing **Knowledge**… knowledge gives you the power to enjoy the sport and ultimately, to be successful.

What's it all about?…

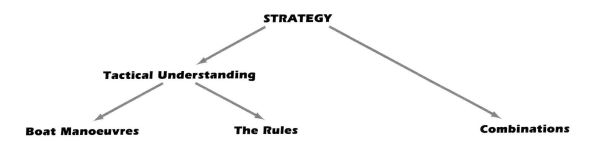

1

TEAM RACING KNOWLEDGE

Sailboat team racing is especially outstanding in terms of the size of the mental challenge that it presents. It is unparalleled in the sailing world in terms of tactical intensity and it draws out the most tenacious sailing from the participants. It brings to small boat sailing the focus of a team game and a higher level of complexity than normal sailing, while drawing on organisational, coaching and umpiring skills. When properly arranged it is also great fun to watch.

All sailors enjoy winning. In addition successful team racers enjoy trying to control their opponents on the water, and socialising with them off the water.

If you have yet to try team racing I hope this book will act as your guide to a new fun activity. If you have experience of the sport I hope the book will enhance your interest and provide you with a systematic framework for improvement. Maybe, like so many before you, you will find team racing carries with it a special passion for life.

1.1 CHARACTERISTICS OF TEAM RACING

The key characteristics of team racing are:
❍ Racing between two teams, each team consisting of two or more boats.
❍ The race is scored so that the combined points of the boats on a team form the team score. The lowest team score wins (with 1 point for first, 2 for second and so on).
❍ An individual may improve the team's position during a race either by overtaking one of the opposition's boats or, using tactical control, by slowing down one of the opposition's boats so that a team mate can overtake.

In addition the following basic attributes add purity and fun:
❍ The boats are all as identical as possible and manageable to all participants.
❍ The short races are scored as "wins" and a series

of race wins against one team or against a mixture of teams in a league is used to get a result, emphasising the 'race win' as the key measure of success.
❍ The courses are short enough to keep events fast moving, with the emphasis on a high number of races. Hence it is more fun and raw boatspeed doesn't have time to dominate.
❍ It is essential that the role of protests is minimised; team racing is more about strategy, skills and manoeuvres incorporating successful rule application. The on-the-water result normally counts as the final result. This is made more possible by good sportsmanship and, when available, sensible umpiring or race "observing".

Team racing has now come to be recognised as an international discipline within the sport of sailing. It has an official world championship for three boat teams. It has a great mixture of tradition and club involvement which is now enhanced by national and international co-ordination.

1.2 TYPES OF TEAM RACING

1.2.1 Two-boat racing – Diagram 1.1
This is a simple yet popular version. Its tactical simplicity makes it useful as an introduction and for practising manoeuvres.

The scoring tie-break system is set so that the team with the last boat loses. This forces the tactics to focus on boat versus boat. Each team mate tries to avoid being in the losing fourth place while firmly pushing the opposition into last if possible. This version is fast moving and often great to watch as it is so easy to see which team is winning.

"Random" two-boat refers to a system where you

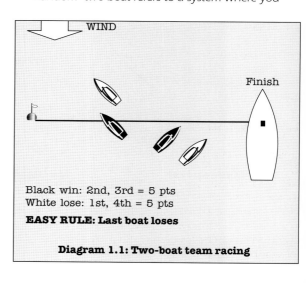

Black win: 2nd, 3rd = 5 pts
White lose: 1st, 4th = 5 pts
EASY RULE: Last boat loses

Diagram 1.1: Two-boat team racing

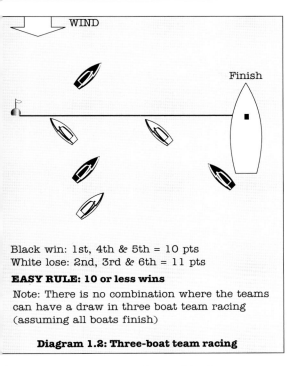

Black win: 1st, 4th & 5th = 10 pts
White lose: 2nd, 3rd & 6th = 11 pts

EASY RULE: 10 or less wins

Note: There is no combination where the teams can have a draw in three boat team racing (assuming all boats finish)

Diagram 1.2: Three-boat team racing

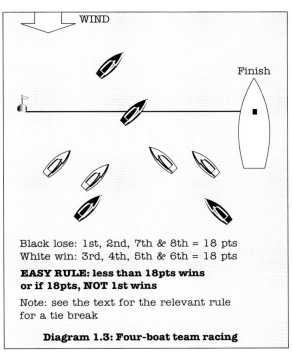

Black lose: 1st, 2nd, 7th & 8th = 18 pts
White win: 3rd, 4th, 5th & 6th = 18 pts

**EASY RULE: less than 18pts wins
or if 18pts, NOT 1st wins**

Note: see the text for the relevant rule for a tie break

Diagram 1.3: Four-boat team racing

change your team mate and opposition for every race. An exciting format with training benefits.

2-Boat Tip: Last Boat Loses

1.2.2 Three-boat racing – Diagram 1.2
This is the most common format and provides a wider variety of winning combinations. The increased number of boats means that there is a high level of interaction between team mates and with the opposition. In addition the increased number of boats means that fast sailing and good fleet racing skills can be well rewarded.

For both 2-boat and 3-boat events the races are often set to be very short (5 to 10 minutes) so that many teams can race each other. Three-boat is the World Championship discipline of the sport.

3-Boat Tip: 1st, 2nd, Anything Wins

1.2.3 Four-boat racing – Diagram 1.3
Eight boats race as two teams of four. The scoring tie-break system of team racing (see below) means that 1, 2, 7, 8, is a losing combination. This format is often used with keelboat racing and has the attraction of involving a large number of people in one race. Races are usually longer than in 2- or 3-boat events. The format is used in some club matches and some institutional trophy events. The premier event is the British-American Cup for which international teams compete.

4-Boat Tip: Three boats in the top four ensures a win for your team

The rules state that "If there is a tie on points the team having the combination of race scores that does not include first place wins". This statement applies to the scoring of all team racing but you can see from the diagrams that it is more relevant to two and four boat team racing.

1.2.4 Why team race?
Many fleet racers do some team racing: it's fun, and is an ideal way to sharpen skills. You will gain place after place in tight fleet races. Team racing has formed part of Olympic training for sailors such as Ben Ainslie.

1.3 TYPES OF EVENT

There are a variety of ways to structure an event. Tables of efficient **round robin** sequences can be obtained through the UK Team Racing Association. In addition to planning the ideal sequence some contingency should be in place for a curtailed event. **Seeding** of round robins and using number of loses instead of wins can help with this. The ISAF rules for deciding tie breaks are specifically detailed in the rules (Team Racing Appendix (D)).

The **knockout** format is usually used at the end of

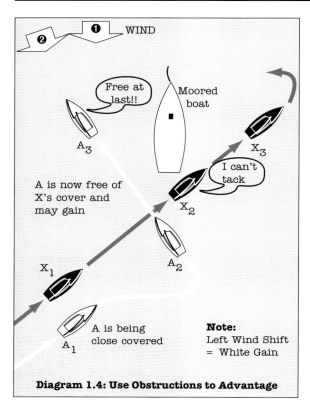

Diagram 1.4: Use Obstructions to Advantage

events as they culminate in multi-race matches between the leading teams. Organisers try to avoid **cutting** to the knockout stage too early as this inevitably then excludes some teams. The knockout stage allows umpiring to be focused on close, championship-critical races.

To keep the racing as close as possible it can be appropriate, in larger competitions, to have a top league and a silver and bronze league. The teams involved in these leagues can have their own final. In some events the winner of the silver league, or repêchage, earns a place in the final knockout stages.

1.4 STRATEGY – SKILL – MANOEUVRE

The words above are emphasised so as to provide both this book and your thinking about the sport with a simple structure. They're the key components. **Decide** on an effective STRATEGY and **use** your SKILLS to **execute** the MANOEUVRES to create a **win**.

STRATEGY is...
❍ the short term intended tactical outcome of a manoeuvre
❍ or, a way of approaching the race or event.
An example of the former is the "Squeeze" – forcing an

opponent behind a team mate, and of the latter 'Boatspeed them!'

SKILL: Is the ability to...
❍ **do** a manoeuvre well, or
❍ **understand** something which is happening, or
❍ **anticipate** the impact of an action.
Examples are 'exert your windshadow on another boat', 'see and anticipate the effect of a windshift on the fleet' and 'stop at a mark and judge when to start sailing fast again'.

MANOEUVRE: Execute an action. It is...
❍ immediate and directed at a specific boat, or
❍ subtle, longer term, developmental and involves several boats.
An example of the first is to 'luff to trap another boat' and of the second is to 'gybe to get to the "inside" on the run'.

A strategy is a framework within which to make tactical decisions on which manoeuvres to attempt. This book will supply you with guidelines, not rules. Team racing really does supply scope for you to express yourself and if your expression shows discipline with flair then it is most likely to be successful.

Part I of the book deals with strategy and skills. Part II deals with the manoeuvres.

1.5 BASIC STRATEGIC CONCEPTS

Strategy is essentially the **overall game plan** for the race, the match, the event or, if you're really serious, the season's campaign.

1.5.1 Examine the Event Format
Is it a round robin or a knockout competition? What is the points system in use (e.g. for penalties and scoring the series) and what other important information is in the Sailing Instructions?

1.5.2 Assess the Sailing Area
The good team racer looks at the geographic features around the racecourse to spot any opportunities to help his own team or hinder the opposition on their way around it. The sort of things to check are highlighted in Diagrams 1.4, 1.5 & 1.6. The importance of **obstructions** is really appreciated when you manage to "trap" another sailor only to find that you have to give them "room" at an obstruction causing you to lose the control you had. As well as these control opportunities there may be wind or tide advantages where one side of the course is either faster or slower or more gusty or shifty. Note these areas, share this knowledge with your team, and use them when deciding on your race tactics.

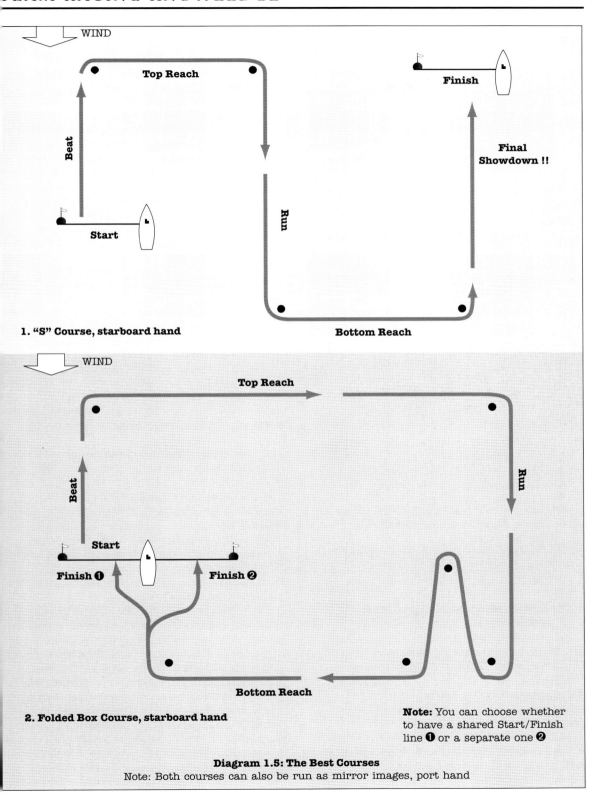

1. "S" Course, starboard hand

2. Folded Box Course, starboard hand

Note: You can choose whether to have a shared Start/Finish line ❶ or a separate one ❷

Diagram 1.5: The Best Courses
Note: Both courses can also be run as mirror images, port hand

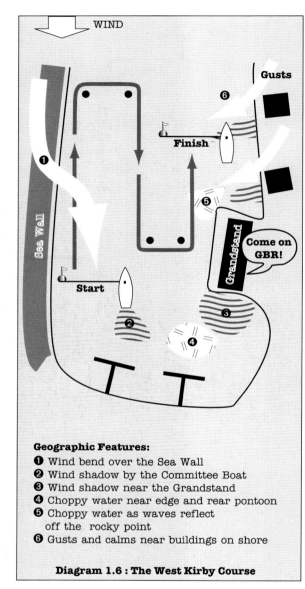

Geographic Features:
① Wind bend over the Sea Wall
② Wind shadow by the Committee Boat
③ Wind shadow near the Grandstand
④ Choppy water near edge and rear pontoon
⑤ Choppy water as waves reflect
   off the rocky point
⑥ Gusts and calms near buildings on shore

Diagram 1.6 : The West Kirby Course

1.5.3 Assess your Team's Strengths & Weaknesses
❑ Crew weight and technique
❑ Starting style and preferences
❑ Sailing style – go fast or be more combative

1.5.4 Assess the Opposition
Assess the Opposition in the same way for their Strengths and Weaknesses.

1.5.5 Assess the Opposition's Expected Strategy
How aggressive do you expect them to be? How will they use what they consider to be their advantages?

1.6 SKILLS
This section covers the **activity on the water**.

1.6.1 Tactical Considerations
1.6.1.1 Winning or losing?
It is often unclear to the sailors who is winning a team race. A helm and crew have to concentrate on sailing the boat. Its then possible to get drawn into a tactical duel which may be unnecessary and threatening to the winning position the team occupies. A good knowledge of the 'combinations' (score options) will soon emerge following a bit of practice. Nobody should have to go around the racecourse adding up the points all the time. Focus on getting boats into sustainable good positions at the front of the race. After the positions in the **top three places** are established it is obvious who is likely to win in three-boat racing. The positions in the top half of the fleet in three boat sailing are usually much more sustainable than, say, a fourth or fifth placing.

   In two-boat races you can simply focus on the **last pair** of boats and see who is in control. If it is not your team in control of this pair then you are in trouble.

   In four-boat team racing it takes longer to establish what your prospects are. There are enough boats to expect significant place changing so the win/lose clarity is often elusive and you have to keep working on your positions and occasionally do some fast maths near the finish line.

Tip: Remember the only combination which really counts is the one you finish in

1.6.1.2 Stable or unstable?
These terms describe the 'type' of combination during a race.
STABLE = The race combination is unlikely to change due to the boat positions where one team is firmly winning (but has not yet won).
UNSTABLE = The race combination is precarious and the final result is therefore uncertain.

   Stable and unstable are terms which refer to the volatility of a particular combination in a team race. That is not a reflection on the personalities involved! It is to do with how opposing boats are interlinked and what actions they are likely to carry out.

   To understand the concept you will need to follow through the normal "overtaking pattern" that emerges when one team starts to manoeuvre against another. The stages I describe in reality often merge together but it will help if the components are understood.

   A team race position change usually follows this pattern:
❍   one boat decides to **compress** the race by

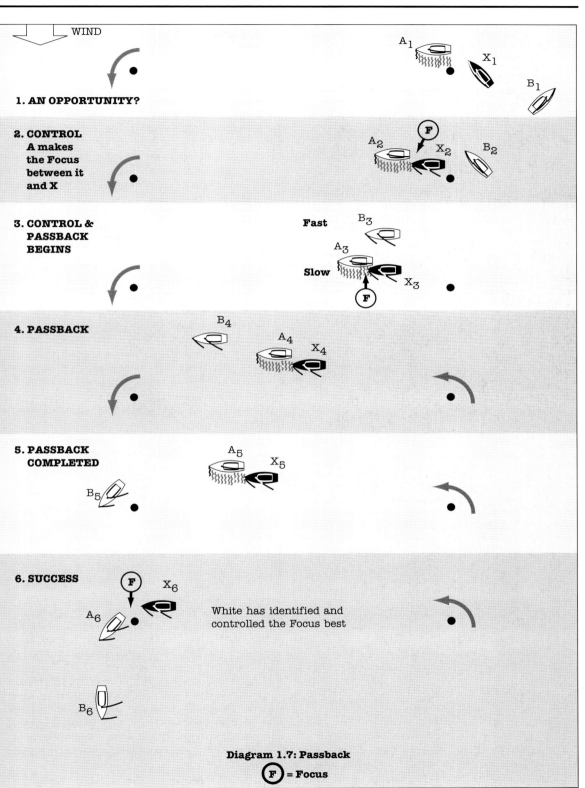

WIND

1. AN OPPORTUNITY?

2. CONTROL
   A makes
   the Focus
   between it
   and X

3. CONTROL &
   PASSBACK
   BEGINS

Fast

Slow

4. PASSBACK

5. PASSBACK
   COMPLETED

6. SUCCESS

White has identified and
controlled the Focus best

Diagram 1.7: Passback

F = Focus

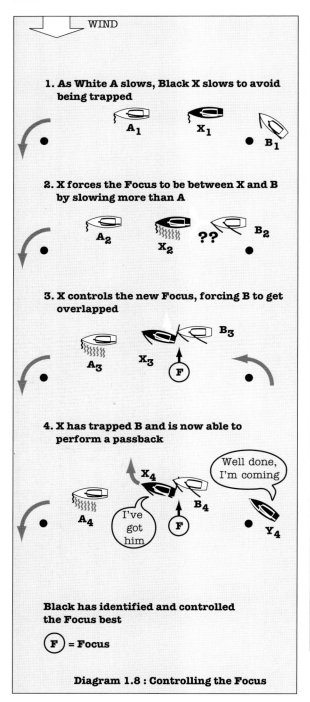

1. As White A slows, Black X slows to avoid being trapped

2. X forces the Focus to be between X and B by slowing more than A

3. X controls the new Focus, forcing B to get overlapped

4. X has trapped B and is now able to perform a passback

Well done, I'm coming

I've got him

Black has identified and controlled the Focus best

(F) = Focus

Diagram 1.8 : Controlling the Focus

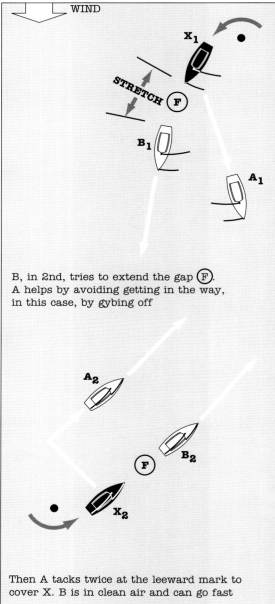

B, in 2nd, tries to extend the gap (F). A helps by avoiding getting in the way, in this case, by gybing off

Then A tacks twice at the leeward mark to cover X. B is in clean air and can go fast

Diagram 1.9: Stretch

slowing the boat behind it.

○ as the boats get closer together it becomes easier to see an overtaking opportunity for any boats astern. At this point the initiating, leading boat seeks to **control** what is happening, for example by preventing the enemy boat astern from tacking or by slowing them with windshadow.

○ the **passback** now takes place. This refers to the moment when the team mate boat sails around the pair of boats and is therefore promoted two places while the opposition boat loses one place (Diagram 1.7).

1.6.1.3 'Team' or 'Fleet'

The boat-on-boat tactics associated with deliberately manoeuvring your boat to **slow down** the opposition, to the benefit of your team mates, is the traditional view of "team" tactics. In "team" mode the boats will be close together trying to get control or evade being pushed where they don't want to go. Passbacks will occur and boats will stop or slow at turning marks.

In "fleet" mode the sailors are working their way round the course **quickly**, going at full speed and maximising the use of any tactical advantages such as windshifts. This is the approach taken by the team when they are not threatened by the opposition in the immediate future, either because they are far ahead or far behind or because the boats have become separated across the course by some distance. In the circumstances where a team mate starts struggling for position a sailor in 'fleet' mode would be poised ready to go back into close quarter team tactics if required. At the start of a race, the positions are often unclear and most boats race as fast as possible until a combination emerges.

Sailing well in 'team mode' requires a great deal of concentration and it can be difficult to spot moments when your best weapon might be to switch into 'fleet mode' and go as fast as possible. It is usual for unstable combinations to result in a great deal of team tactics and as a consequence the boats will progress more slowly round the course.

The good team will be **flexible** but **co-ordinated** across the team as to whether they are trying to go fast or slowly. Often, for a particular race scenario, it can pay to make sure your team mates and yourself agree on this point and communicate your view. It can be worth hailing words of encouragement to either engage the opposition (team) or to just get on with sailing fast (fleet).

Top Tip: It is also important that crew and helm communicate and work together on what their boat is doing. For example, "we're slowing", "flap!", "speed", "max speed!" are good prompts

Some teams define specific boats to be more team or fleet orientated depending on their particular skills, while the 'complete' team racer is good at both! It is more likely that what you do will be dictated by your position in a combination.

Two-boat team racing tends to result in more "team" tactics. Three-boat racing puts a strong emphasis on being able to switch to the most appropriate mode quickly. Four-boat is more "fleet" orientated although can shift dramatically to team tactics near the end of unstable races.

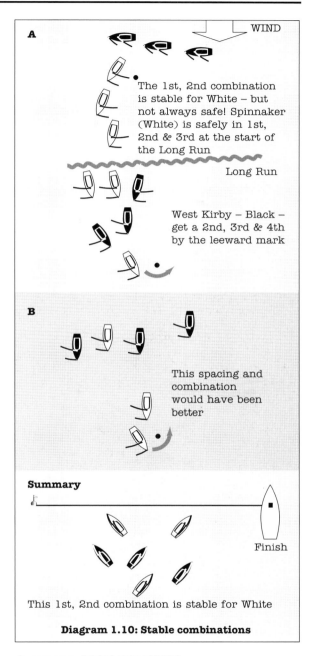

A   WIND

The 1st, 2nd combination is stable for White – but not always safe! Spinnaker (White) is safely in 1st, 2nd & 3rd at the start of the Long Run

Long Run

West Kirby – Black – get a 2nd, 3rd & 4th by the leeward mark

B

This spacing and combination would have been better

Summary

Finish

This 1st, 2nd combination is stable for White

Diagram 1.10: Stable combinations

Summary: BASIC CONCEPTS

Winning	←→	Losing
Stable	←→	Unstable
'Team'	←→	'Fleet'

1.6.1.4 Focus

The F with a circle around it has been used in the diagrams to mark the **CONTROL FOCUS** of the race. The focus may be a particular boat (for example X) which

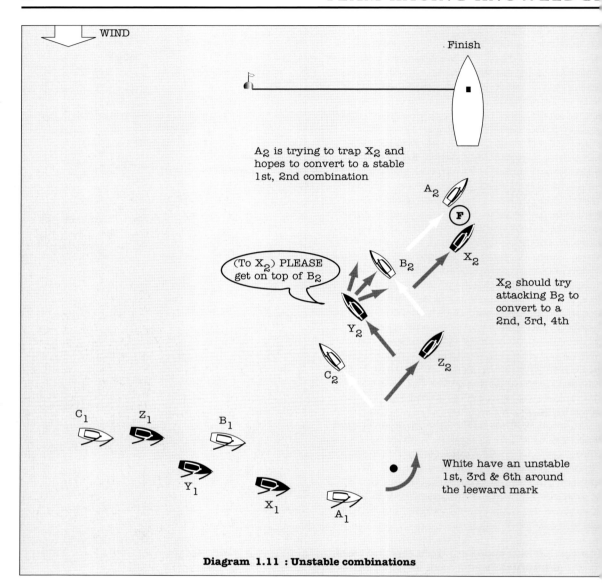

Diagram 1.11 : Unstable combinations

is the key component in converting the combination to a better one or it may be used to refer to a **GAP** between two boats over which the teams will battle for control. Control may involve **trapping** and **slowing**, or **extending** away. Which you try to do will depend on your combination. The gap in Diagram 1.8 is just such a focus for the race in question. This concept of a focus is a useful one for identifying where the action needs to happen. This means the team is more likely to know what they are trying to achieve, because as you can see there is a need to **work together**.

In the run up to the COMPRESS manoeuvres described in Diagram 1.7, boat X will be trying to get closer to B by "trapping" her in 3rd place so she is unable to do the

over-take required to make the 1st , 2nd combination. This effort by X will also bring the whole race back together so the overall distance from 6th to 1st will decrease, which increases the chance of an upset.

Naturally B might also realise that the FOCUS for this team is going to be the passback manoeuvre on X, so he stays back a bit allowing A to trap X before X can trap B. In Diagram 1.8, X controls the Focus best and traps B. In reality, success will depend on who compresses, controls and passes back most effectively.

Tip: The boat/team that identifies the control focus first, gains the initiative

The winning team now attempts to consolidate its position. For example, by stretching the race out so that it is harder for boats to change their race position.

In order to explain the "stretch" part of this process more clearly, let us now suppose that this successful manoeuvre (exactly which manoeuvre it is is unimportant at the moment, the principle is what counts) results in a winning 1st and 2nd combination for the White team. Their second boat (who initiated the successful passback) is now very close to the enemy boat behind. This means there is a risk that this boat may get past, perhaps by getting an overlap at a mark or doing a better tack. The 2nd boat (B) therefore decides to **make the situation less risky**. It sails fast and **stretches** out the race so there is **as big a gap as possible** where the race focus lies, which in this example is between B and X (see Diagram 1.9).

Before I understood this concept our team (from the Spinnaker Club) were leading a Wilson Trophy race with a 1, 2, 3 combination. We went onto a run in this supposedly stable winning combination and promptly got sailed past by the West Kirby team who achieved a 2, 3, 4 combination by the leeward mark. If we had realised that the stable combination needed to be **defended** by stretching out the race, the result might have been different (see Diagram 1.10A). This stretching could have been achieved by our third boat stopping at the windward mark. This would have slowed the approaching West Kirby boats and allowed our two leading boats clearer air for the run (Diagram 1.10B).

The term STABLE therefore refers to a combination where the boats of the two teams are clearly separated in the race order. Boats will have to **overtake from behind** to affect the team positions so there is less chance of a passback being achieved or even being necessary. A stable race will be characterised by a team holding a winning combination where the FOCUS is a gap between boats that the leading team will be trying to extend or stretch (Diagram 1.10). This does not mean it is unassailable.

The term UNSTABLE, by contrast, depicts the situation where opposing boats are **sandwiched** between one another (Diagram 1.11). Here the FOCUS may well be a boat which one team is trying to passback and both teams may have several options available to them to try and either make a winning combination more secure or to try and reverse the scores from a current losing combination. The 1, 3, 6 combination for White A, B, C in Diagram 1.11 is a very good example of an unstable winning combination. It would be hard to predict which team will come out on top. An unstable race makes for great entertainment value!

1.6.1.5 "Mind the Gap" – The Push-Pull Effect
This strategy is very important to the management of

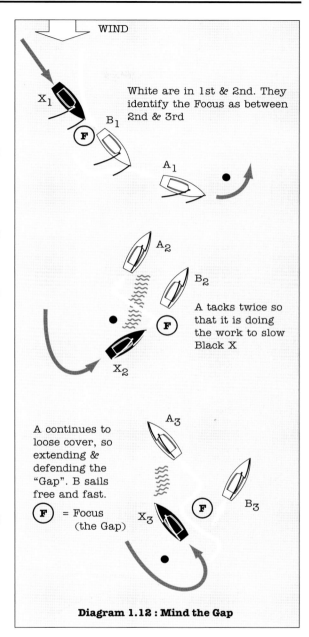

White are in 1st & 2nd. They identify the Focus as between 2nd & 3rd

A tacks twice so that it is doing the work to slow Black X

A continues to loose cover, so extending & defending the "Gap". B sails free and fast.

F = Focus (the Gap)

Diagram 1.12 : Mind the Gap

combinations (see Part I – Stable and Unstable Combinations).

A UK coach pointed out that there is an even simpler way of reminding yourself of what really matters. He summarises this using the well known London Underground phrase of "Mind The Gap!" Essentially this means you should identify where in the combination there is a critical gap. Do you, as a team, want to attack the gap, by closing up or overtaking, or do you need to defend the gap, by opening out or maintaining the

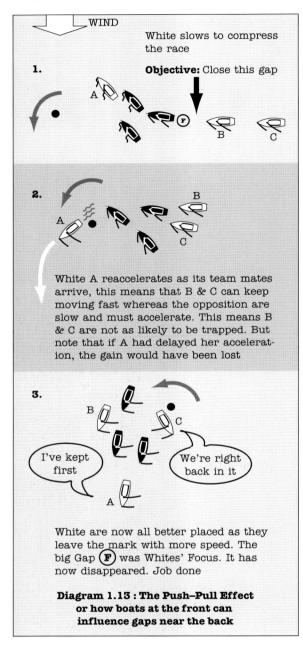

WIND

White slows to compress the race

1.

Objective: Close this gap

A

F

B

C

2.

B

A

C

White A reaccelerates as its team mates arrive, this means that B & C can keep moving fast whereas the opposition are slow and must accelerate. This means B & C are not as likely to be trapped. But note that if A had delayed her acceleration, the gain would have been lost

3.

B

C

I've kept first

We're right back in it

A

White are now all better placed as they leave the mark with more speed. The big Gap **F** was Whites' Focus. It has now disappeared. Job done

Diagram 1.13 : The Push–Pull Effect or how boats at the front can influence gaps near the back

the race boats are almost like railway carriages in that the lead boat's speed will directly impact on those boats behind it. This is true as boats slow on a reach, as they close up to each other and try to avoid overlaps. It is also true at marks when boats slow because they are reluctant to go around the outside and are not permitted to barge through on the inside. This 'virtual linkage' of the boats is something lead boats should be sensitive to. While stopping to compress the fleet is often a desirable manoeuvre there is also a **right moment to start accelerating** again so that there is less chance of your team mates behind finding life difficult. Diagram 1.13 illustrates this point.

Minding the gap means, in particular, both controlling and appreciating the size of it. It is obvious (but not always appreciated) that a big gap will take longer to close up. Team racing boats have the power to 'stop' boats by their manoeuvres. Gaps will yo-yo between being very big and very small.

When a race is close, how you control the critical gaps is the secret key to the whole sport… and now you know about it as well!

1.6.1.6 Time – the other dimension
Team Racing is a three-dimensional sport in the sense that TIME is a dimension. A key input to the tactical decisions is the **remaining time available** as you sail to the finish line. This is all the time and opportunity you will have to change the combination (Diagram 1.14).

As a losing team gets nearer to the finish they will attempt to pull off more desperate manoeuvres. The astute team will therefore look at the number of legs to be sailed in advance of a race and assess the **best opportunities** to carry out team manoeuvres. In particular they will look at the legs and marks just before the finish in case they find there is still a passback to be done before the finish.

A team which has a very weak position may opt for desperate tactics early on because they know that time is unlikely to improve their position. This concept of 'time remaining' also makes it important to have a "finish" when practising, in order to force extreme tactics to try and achieve a team win before you reach the finish line.

1.6.1.7 Balance and leverage – Diagram 1.15
This tactical concept refers to the contrast in circumstances between having a carefully balanced seesaw where two people are both up in the air (balance) and the same seesaw having the pivot point moved towards one end, when the person at the longer end comes down to the ground.

Now consider a racecourse where two boats are close together on a beat near the middle of the course. This is the equivalent of balance on the seesaw. If we

positions? Once you have decided where the gap is and what you need to achieve you will automatically know whether to compress or slow or whether you personally are near the **critical focus** of the race or not. Diagram 1.12 shows how to protect your most vulnerable boat (the boat that needs to go fast) by double tacking at the leeward mark.

If you are further away from the gap you should be conscious of your indirect effect on it. At certain parts of introduce a windshift the boats still remain reasonably close together. If the boats are **separated** by some distance across the course the resulting effect of the windshift (or a gust on one side) can be more dramatic. The further apart the boats get, the more **potential leverage** the boats have on each other.

This then becomes a tactical consideration. If, for example, you need to get past another boat and you think the conditions are shifty you could send one boat to each side of the course. If you are lucky one of your team will get sufficient leverage to get past. This "bang the corner" viewpoint has some risks…

❍ If the beat is long enough a boat playing all the shifts up the middle may do better than one who gets the extremes of good and bad on one side.

❍ If the shift is big you might find you overstand and therefore lose ground.

❍ Your best sailor might go the wrong way and never get back in the race.

My recommendation is to look at getting leverage as a powerful factor in short course racing. Most team racing does take place on short courses where often only one big shift occurs on a single upwind leg. It is particularly important when deciding what to do when pairs of boats from opposing teams split on the course and Part II (Manoeuvres) looks at how **covering** tactics are influenced by leverage and balance across the fleet in just such a case. (See Diagram 1.15.)

1.6.1.8 Attack and control from astern

When sailing in the Hinman Trophy – the US Open Championships – the UK team frequently found itself on the receiving end of the fast sailing of the US teams who are more experienced in Vanguards. On two occasions I used "attack from astern" on the last beat to break down the lead which the US teams had achieved. This strategy entails realising that you have the opportunity to distract an opponent sufficiently well to get you and your team mates back into the race.

The manoeuvres which you can use to achieve this are covered in detail in Part II but here are some examples:

On a beat…

❍ Tempt an enemy boat into a **tacking duel** so that it slows down and either you may get past it or a team mate can overtake both of you. A high frequency of tacks makes a boat handling error more likely.

❍ Encourage an enemy boat (who feels obliged to cover your moves) to follow you off on a bad shift or into a lull while your team mates head for the better breeze. Use the principle of leverage to control this, going further to the side of the beat to make the situation more likely to turn around.

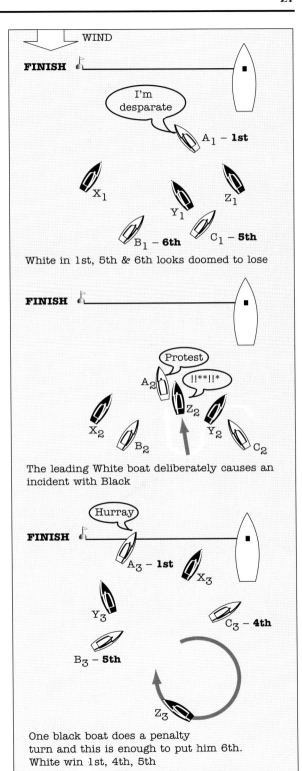

White in 1st, 5th & 6th looks doomed to lose

The leading White boat deliberately causes an incident with Black

One black boat does a penalty turn and this is enough to put him 6th. White win 1st, 4th, 5th

Diagram 1.14 : Last Ditch Options

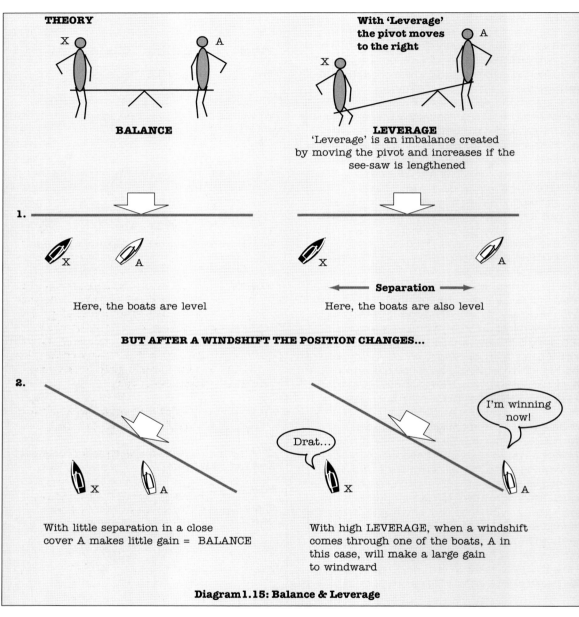

Diagram 1.15: Balance & Leverage

Two of you can do this simultaneously by going in opposite directions.

○ Use **obstructions** (like moored boats, the shore, right-of-way boats and out of position umpire boats) to 'wipe out' an opposition boat who finds its course blocked while you sail on and gain separation from it. This happened at the '98 World Championship held in Miami (see Diagram 1.4).

On the reach...

○ If you have a team mate behind you and an enemy boat in front you are able to attack from behind. By tempting the opposition boat to luff you by deliberately sailing to windward of them you can take a big course deviation and allow your team mate to sail through (this is called the high/low manoeuvre).

At marks...

○ Despite being behind you may be able to **get an inside overlap** which will entitle you to 'room' at the mark. The rules and tactics concerning this are covered later but you should be aware from fleet racing that an overlap gained before the two length zone can then allow you to round the mark on the inside and gain a handsome lead on the opposition boat as it is forced to round wide.

On the run...

○ When behind you are well placed to make use of advantageous gusts and shifts before they are available to the opposition ahead of you. This can often result in a big gain and allow you to **blanket** them, and with good positioning and gybing you are in a very strong position to overtake. The run provides such a good opportunity that many race organisers make sure there is a run in the course to keep the racing even closer and more exciting for everybody.

1.6.1.9 Preparing your strategy

A number of tactical considerations can be identified in advance. They involve an examination of the relative skills across the team and also the skills of the opposition team members.

Particular team members may also be allocated a particular "role" within the strategy. Examples could include…

○ Take out their fast guy before the start
○ Avoid confrontation and go for speed
○ Take a particular end on the start

Or they may be team approaches such as...

○ Avoid incidents and go for speed
○ Build a winning position with small safe moves
○ Attack early and hard to make a stable winning combination
○ Do match race starts by pairing off

It is important that you take the time to devise a pre-agreed strategy together before going on the water. The team should agree how to approach the race; to say nothing is very confident indeed or means the team already has a standard plan for this particular team or type of team. The check list below can help prompt ideas for your pre-agreed strategy.

Team Strategy Check List:

❑ Assess individual strengths and weaknesses

❑ Assess team strengths and weaknesses

❑ Assess the sailing area, course and conditions

❑ Examine the event format

❑ Assess the opposition's strengths and weaknesses

❑ Assess the opposition's expected strategy

This aspect of the 'gameplan' is therefore the critical link between preparation and the race itself. Many teams fail to realise there is an opportunity to gain an advantage here.

The overall tactical approach has many contributing components. I have put the main inputs in the Summary of Key Tactical Features below. It is a useful exercise to look at a race scenario as a team and highlight to each other the key information components both before and after racing, trying to judge if you anticipated correctly what the main factors were going to be. An example of getting this wrong would be saying "we are faster than them, just sail loose (low risk)" only to find that a new guy on their team has revolutionised their speed.

1.6.1.10 Three boat racing combinations

In this section I'll look at the "combination options" to supply a strategy to act as a framework for manoeuvres. As it isn't always clear what positions boats are in you might have to assess how you think they might come together and make your judgement of the resulting race combination. Your strategy will also be strongly influenced by the spacing of the boats, which can present a useful tool. By increasing the gap you create a buffer and make overtaking less likely. By reducing the gap you make control more likely and place changing possible.

Top tip: If you are not sure of the combination keep sailing fast. If in doubt go fast

Selected combinations are looked at from the perspective of the White team. A, B & C comprise the WHITE team, X, Y & Z comprise the BLACK team and F is the FOCUS (the critical gap). In graphics of the Combinations, the action is divided into **Before**, **During** and **After** – so as to avoid confusion they mean:

Before = The race order before any action.
During = What the White team should be attempting to achieve.
After = The race order after successful action.

The recommended action for White described in this Combinations Section has a "Play" code. These are used by some teams to communicate their intentions in simple terms:

Play "A" = Attack the Front
Play "B" = Beat 2 of their boats (i.e., 2, 3, 4)
Play "C" = Try the 1, 4, 5

Note: There are only 3 different plays to think about.

Combination: 1st, 2nd, 3rd   Play "A"

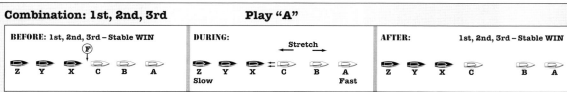

Note: It is nice to win with a 1, 2, 3 but unless you protect the position as above you may well end up losing despite a good start to the race. C in 3rd stretches the race by slowing the back half, so allowing team mates in 1st and 2nd to get away. C has controlled the critical focus.

Combination: 1st, 2nd, 4th   Play "A"

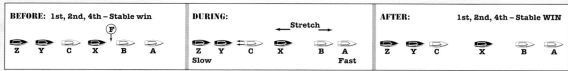

Note: A & B make sure they stay ahead and get away if they can. C tries to obstruct all the opposition's boats around him. When A & B break away it is not uncommon for their positions to change round on a beat as they work together and keep some separation between them. A & B work together to defend the focus by opening out the gap with X.

    With a 1, 2, 4 it can sometimes pay to do a passback and get a 1, 2, 3. This will depend on the circumstances. It may be the best action if 3rd is very strong and needs to be neutralised before the boats start a long run.

Combination: 1st, 2nd, 5th or 1st, 2nd, 6th   Play "A"

Same as 1, 2, 4 except it will rarely pay to attempt to get the last White boat back into the picture. Concentrate on the 1st, 2nd. With any 1st, 2nd combination the focus will always be between 2nd and 3rd, but other boats may affect the gap indirectly.

Combination: 1st, 3rd, 4th   Play "A"

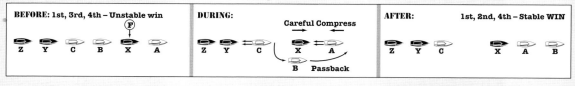

Note: A traps X who is in 2nd place. This brings B closer and then allows B to pass and go into 1st place forcing X to 3rd. There is no rush here as B and C are close behind X and one of them will come past easily. Any over-aggressive slowing of the race by A might bring Y and Z in 5th and 6th back into the action which is not at all what White want to happen. If A is not confident it would be better to do this manoeuvre on a beat where B and C can sail around easily. It may pay for C to concentrate on keeping Y and Z out of the game while A and B work on the passback but this will depend on the spacing.

Combination: 1st, 3rd, 5th or 1st, 3rd, 6th

Note: It will often pay to do just the same as for a 1st, 3rd, 4th. As the last White boat gets further back in the race it is a more vulnerable position for White because the leading Black boat (X) will try to attack B with less risk of this allowing C through.

Combination: 1st, 4th, 5th – Option A – HOLD   Play "C"

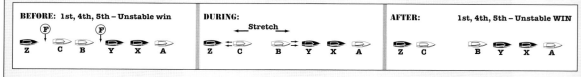

Note: This is a hazardous but winning combination for White. As shown above they all try to stay in their positions. To do this C stops Z and keeps her in 6th. B tries to keep the game moving and A keeps first. The visible effect of this is that a gap will emerge between 4th and 5th as they concentrate their efforts forwards and backwards respectively. B & C control the gaps with the opposition (ahead of B and behind C). Reality is that the boats will spread out on a beat or run and things are bound to change.

First place becomes safer (and therefore 1st can afford to take risks) after the final run. Up until then 2nd/3rd have the whip hand.

Top Tip: A large 4th/5th gap makes a safer 1st, 4th, 5th combination so 5th should normally attack the opponent in 6th.

Combination: 1st, 4th, 5th – Option B – Attack at the front   Play "A"

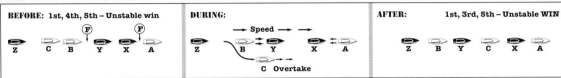

Note: In this option, B keeps Y busy from behind with "distraction" tactics, A stops X from getting involved and C sails fast to overtake the boats ahead. The difference from the strategy above is that White are attacking the front of the race trying to get two boats in the front half of the fleet rather than just trying to sustain their positions defensively.

Which of the two 1st, 4th, 5th strategies you prefer to do will depend on circumstances. Typically the 'attack the front' method will work best for a situation with plenty of time left whereas the defensive "hold 1st, 4th… GAP… 5th" method is most commonly used later in the race. You should look at 2, 3, 6 below since this is the other team's view of the same combination.

Combination: 1st, 4th, 6th   Play "A"

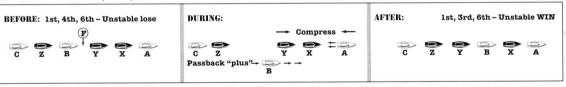

Note: This is getting really tricky for White. Still keeping 1st, White attempts to compress the front half of the race so that her team mate in 4th can get through to 3rd, and hopefully better. This option again implies attacking the front and the extra passback will probably need a special opportunity such as a mark to stop or slow at, because Y, ahead, has a natural advantage controlling the focus with B.

Alternatively… 1st, 4th, 6th   Play "C"

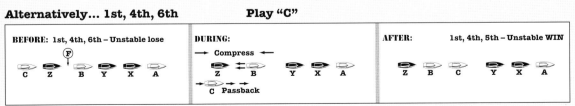

Note: This seems simpler because the passback is easier since B has more control over the focus with Z. Unfortunately there is no right answer. This 1st, 4th, 5th option is a good idea if the first boats have virtually finished because in that situation A will have little opportunity to help. If however the race has plenty of time left then the 1st, 4th, 5th will prove to be difficult to hold. In this combination all the boats must know what the team objective is, should they be attacking the front or doing a passback. This is a useful area for there to be a team "call" as to which to do.

Combination: 1st, 5th, 6th   **Play "A", Wait for Play "C" / "B" options**

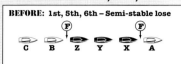
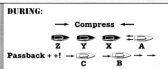
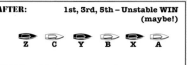

Note: This is difficult for White because there are two points of focus. Things to try include a good mark trap by A, perhaps allowing C and B into a position to attack from behind (e.g., on a run or using leverage on a beat). A should try to keep 1st because late in the race a 1st, 4th, 5th will be an option. A should try to compress the race.

Combination: 2nd, 3rd, 4th   **Play "B"**

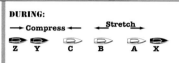
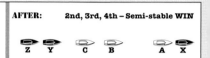

Note: As with the converse 1st, 5th, 6th, the battle here is on two fronts but White, with its 3 boats together in 2nd, 3rd, 4th can be better organised than Black. By working together they can protect this semi-stable combination all the way to the finish. Black X is left not sure what to do. If X attacks very hard then White may switch to PLAY "A".

Combination: 2nd, 3rd, 5th   **Play "B"**

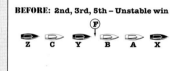
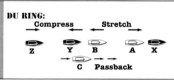
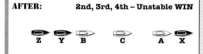

Note: Despite being a winning combination this is very dangerous for White. B and C need to do a passback to promote C up to 3rd or 4th and past the potentially troublesome Y in 4th place before the fun starts. As in the 2nd, 3rd, 4th combination, the lead White boat, A, in 2nd place tries to keep X out of the action so that the White team can act as a combined force whereas Black suffers fighting a battle on two fronts.

Combination: 2nd, 3rd, 6th   **Play "A"**

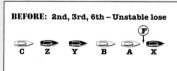
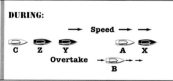
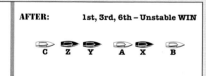

Note: This is an attack the front option for this combination. A and B work together to get one of them past X and into 1st place. If there is plenty of sailing time and therefore opportunities left then there is some hope of doing this. If however the race is nearing its end we need to turn and look for a quicker passback option…

Combination: 2nd, 3rd, 6th   **Play "B"**

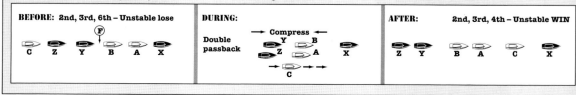

Notes: In this alternative A and B take on Y and Z and occupy them to the extent that C is allowed to sail past them gaining the team a winning combination. The reality of doing this is that B in 3rd will trap Y in 4th while A in 2nd has to decide when to dive down and take on Z in 5th – this being a brave and difficult decision, since it will feel to A like he is throwing away hard earned places as he goes back. By trapping the opposition in these two pairs in a synchronised and balanced way C in 6th is released to sail merrily through into 2nd. This gives the team the 2nd, 3rd, 4th they have been looking for. Well at least as long as X does not decide to start doing something!

This combination really emphasises "ATTACK BEFORE YOU ARE ATTACKED".

Combination: 2nd, 4th, 5th   Play "B"

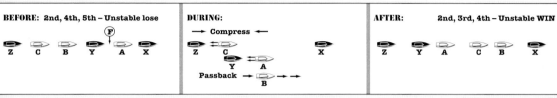

Note: A has to get busy here, first doing a passback to promote B up the fleet while C makes sure Z stays last. This is a winning 2nd, 3rd, 5th combination but the White team goes to the next stage as well (they are pretty good!). Next B (or A) repeats and does a passback to get C through. A is going to have to be good to fight off the attentions of X, although if X does close right in on A she should stick on Y because this would give B and C a chance to sail around them all.

Combination: 2nd, 4th, 6th   Play "B"

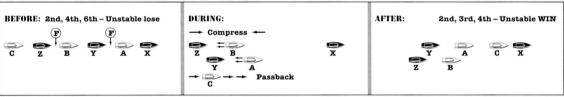

Note: In this combination the White team have to work together to bring C through. A and B must control Y and Z simultaneously.

NEARLY ALL WINNING COMBINATIONS INVOLVE TWO OF YOUR TEAM BEING IN THE TOP THREE

The only exception to this is the 1st, 4th, 5th combination (see above). "Two in top three" is a good objective to remember when your position looks poor. It is not useful to all work on small improvements in position when what you really need to do is overtake from behind and get more boats into the front of the fleet.

Combination: 2nd, 5th, 6th   Play "B"

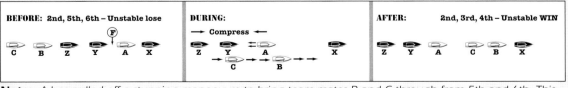

Note: A has pulled off a stunning manoeuvre to bring team mates B and C through from 5th and 6th. This is likely to require a good "mark trap" by A hopefully forcing one of the opposing team to commit a foul. Even if this is only partially successful it is a positive move as long as the White team keep 2nd place. The 2nd, 5th, 6th combination is extremely dangerous for White and they need to take action as soon as possible. If X is a useful sailor A can expect to find things very difficult so should attack and get emphatic control over the focus with Y & Z.

Combination: 3rd, 4th, 5th   Play "A"

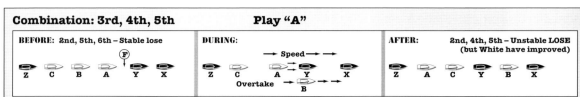

Note: Attack the front. It is no good at all just trying to win a rearguard action here. White must use all their guile to get a boat into the top two positions. The most likely way of achieving this is for A to use "distraction" tactics such as getting Y to engage in a close cover. This will help B to get through. Good skills (see next section) will be vital to White's success here.

Combination: 3rd, 4th, 6th   Play "A"

This is the same as for 3rd, 4th, 5th because the action is in the top three boats. White have got to break into the top two so the 6th or 5th boat are well away from the focus of this race. Any incidents at the back of the race might be good for fun but will not become relevant until the stable Black combination is broken. It will then become very useful for White to come through at the back as well. Boats in this sort of desperate combination will be looking for some risky options like getting right out to one side of a beat to gain from a shift.

Combination: 3rd, 5th, 6th   Play "A"

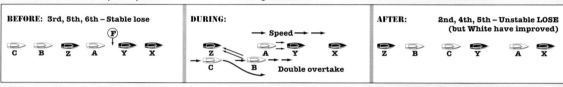

Note: Here B distracts Z allowing C to improve to 4th making the back half of the race unstable and bringing a second White boat into a position to help influence the tactics at the front of the race. A in third place is the critical player and cannot afford to help B or C get through (they must manage that themselves) but must concentrate on staying close to Y. In the optimistic scenario shown above A goes one better than that by overtaking Y and really starting to put Black back under pressure. White as shown are doing well to break a stable combination against them, it may seem unrealistic (until you have practised the skills to use) but this is actually how a strong team will break through and create an unstable situation from a seemingly stable combination against them. Once the race is unstable then far more options emerge.

Combination: 4th, 5th, 6th   Play "A"

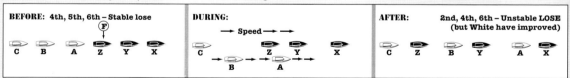

Note: You may think it is unlikely but White look like they may turn this race round because they concentrate on forcing one boat up into the top two as quickly as possible; i.e., they do not focus on getting a 3rd, 4th, 5th, since that is not much use and is still a long way from a win. The best chance of a quick fix to this problem is one or two of the White team taking a "flier". This is an opportunity to visit corner city, to do the one tack beat and see if you have judged that big shift correctly. Look at running skills as well to see if some group blanketing tactics can shoot one boat through to the front.

DON'T GIVE UP

Knowledge of the combinations will help structure your tactical thinking. They will not control your actions. There are many other factors in deciding what to do in a race. This is your "health warning" for this section.
Do not look at "combinations" in isolation

1.6.1.11 SUMMARY OF KEY TACTICAL FEATURES

There are four main tactical inputs which we have looked at in this chapter. Some reminders of what to think about are included below:

WHERE ON RACE TRACK

- ❍ What leg are you on, what legs are coming up?
- ❍ What mark roundings are coming up?
- ❍ Are the boats well split with high leverage?
- ❍ Are the boats close together with balance?
- ❍ Are there any special features (obstructions, another race)?
- ❍ Geographic features such as wind bends, topographic effects or tide variance?

TIME REMAINING *versus* SIZE OF TASK

- ❍ How big a gap is there to close up?
- ❍ How many laps, legs and marks remain?
- ❍ How long is the last leg of the race?

CURRENT RACE POSITION

- ❍ Are you winning or losing?
- ❍ Is the combination stable or unstable?
- ❍ Who is controlling the focus of the race?
- ❍ Is there more than one focus in the race?

PRE-AGREED STRATEGY

- ❍ What were the results of your strategy checks?
- ❍ Compare your strengths and weaknesses within the team and vs opposition. For instance…
  - ❑ speed
  - ❑ rules knowledge
  - ❑ ability to cope under pressure

- ❍ What ground rules have you agreed? For instance…
  - ❑ attack early and get a stable combination
  - ❑ avoid confrontation and go for speed
  - ❑ build a winning position with safe moves

If you can understand the answers to these questions you can use the tactical information gained to help determine what to do in the race. It will be even more useful if you are able to prioritise the factors contributing towards the overall race strategy.

WINNING TEAM TACTICS

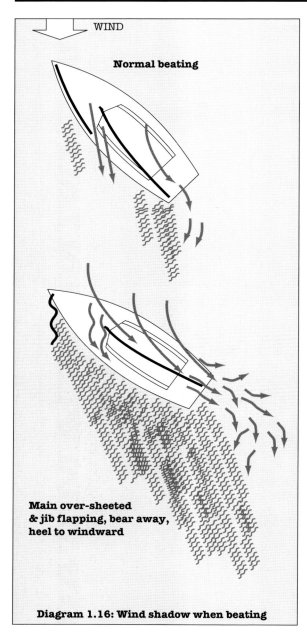

WIND

Normal beating

**Main over-sheeted
& jib flapping, bear away,
heel to windward**

Diagram 1.16: Wind shadow when beating

1.6.1.12 Tactical Commandments: Do's & Don'ts

○ DO identify the focus of the race and attempt to control it.

○ DO compress the race when losing.

○ DO to the boat astern what the boat ahead is doing to you.

○ DO attack before being attacked when the race is unstable.

○ DO concentrate on the size of the important gaps between boats.

○ DON'T be satisfied until the combination is stable

○ DON'T be too risky until near the finish.

○ DON'T let one opponent occupy two of you for too long.

○ DON'T expect team telepathy, communicate your tactics.

○ DON'T get too tied up with one opponent and lose the overview.

The phrases above highlight some tactical tips. The main tactical patterns do repeat themselves. Good teams tend to attack before getting attacked so that they get the initiative, and you can draw the analogy of all competitive team games where so often "surprise" or prompt action gains the swing of play. In team racing there is the earliest possible opportunity to get the initiative, which is the start. In a later section the particular team skills of starting are examined.

A good team does try and get an early stable combination in a race. They use mark traps and boatspeed to good effect and at the right times. The team knows whether they are winning or not and works together to "stretch" the race, particularly when winning, or to "compress" the race if they are losing, and when they need to encourage some place changing. The good team readily identifies the "focus" of the race and either **attacks** it or **defends** it depending on whether they are losing or winning.

The good team have a clear view of the tactical importance of their current race positions or "combination" and the vital consideration of assessing the time remaining in a race against the size of the task facing the team.

1.6.2 Boat positioning skills

Good quality skills allow a wide repertoire of manoeuvres to be performed successfully and consistently. This will build confidence and form a basis for a well understood way of managing the tactics within the team. By contrast a low skill level and frequent mistakes makes the whole team unsettled, although it is not the only factor in the race.

In this section we'll look at some specific skills which exist beyond those skills simply required to fleet race around the course. Everyone can work on improving their skills and expect to see satisfying results.

As a team manager you might use this section as:

○ a checklist for individual or team skills

○ a prompt for practice and coaching ideas

Remember that if you lose a race it is good to approach it as a challenge. The challenge is to identify the skills gaps which cost you the race and to look at ways of working on them. There are probably better moments to do this analysis than straight after a momentous defeat!

1.6.2.1 Windshadow control

Closehauled

To make the downwind zone of disturbed air from a close-hauled boat stronger and larger (see Diagram 1.16):

-) Over-sheet the mainsail so the leech is very tight and stalled out
-) Bear away so the sail is even more over-trimmed for the angle the boat is sailing
-) Intermittently release the jib so it flaps and the "slot" between main and jib is disrupted further
-) Heel the boat to windward to "dig" the top of the rig into the wind to increase the shadow and to increase the effect to the windward side of the boat's track
-) Position yourself on the windward bow of the opponent: closer = more effect.

Reaching

The principle employed is exactly the same on a reach. Over-sheeting the main gives the maximum amount of stalled air for your opponent to try and sail through. The skill here is being able to make the hole in the wind so big that the opposing boat will slow to your speed. This requires a big effort at the right moment. If you start the windshadow too early you will slow too much and you risk being overtaken by the other boat who is prepared and can go above or much further below. When carried out in a reasonable breeze the additional leverage of the over-sheeted sail will require more hiking out. Having slowed down… wait until the boat commits to go below you and then start the aggressive stalling process, steadily increasing the oversheeting (and intermittent jib flapping) as the leeward boat slows. See Diagram 1.17.

Running

If you are trying to catch an opponent on the run the 'close to' windward position offers the maximum windshadow but it is rarely used because you can easily be luffed.

The skill with using your windshadow on the run is to be able to sail down the leeward side of the opposing boat projecting as much of your sail plan over theirs as possible. This is best achieved by heeling the boat to windward and holding the jib out goosewinged. If you carry out the manoeuvre on starboard you are protected from a gybe by the other boat (since he would gybe onto give-way port tack). In addition, as you progress down his leeward side, Rule 11 obliges the overlapped boat to windward to keep clear. This obligation will include him luffing to stop the overtaking boat to leeward sailing into his

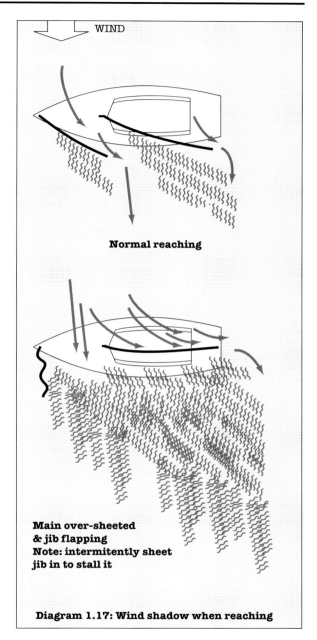

Normal reaching

Main over-sheeted & jib flapping
Note: intermitently sheet jib in to stall it

Diagram 1.17: Wind shadow when reaching

mainsheet. I say this with the warning that there is an obligation on the leeward boat not to approach so close or so fast that the new windward boat is unable to keep clear despite responding promptly in a seamanlike way.

Other considerations on the run include working with a team mate to make your combined windshadows stronger and restrict the options for the boat to "slide" off in one direction or another (see Diagram 1.18).

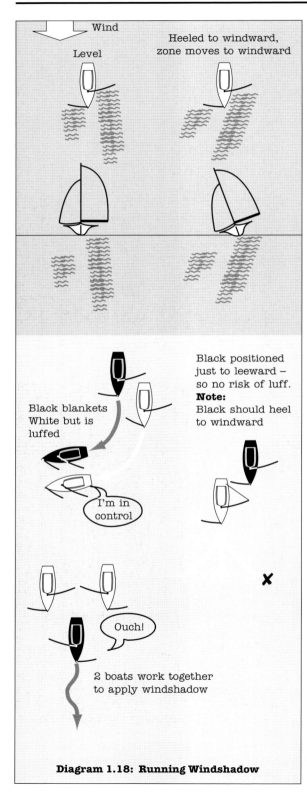

Diagram 1.18: Running Windshadow

1.6.2.2 How to slow down

1. Easing the sails is the simplest way of slowing when close to the wind. Maintain steerage way and keep just enough forward movement to stop the foils stalling out completely. Easing the sails carries the disadvantage of reducing the windshadow effect.

2. Use rudder movement to slow the boat deliberately. Force the rudder to "full lock" in one direction, hold for a few seconds and then reverse the angle.

3. Oversheet the sails. It is the only way to make the sails lose their power once the sailing angle is very broad.

4. Move far aft in the boat causing the stern to dig in. This is useful when stopping in the two-length zone at a leeward mark.

5. Back the mainsail to windward or to leeward: these are very quick ways of stopping a boat. Be careful not to go through head-to-wind or to start going astern or you will become vulnerable to other boats who will gain right-of-way over you. This can be useful for emergency manoeuvering during pre-start or at windward marks.

Whatever slowing methods are being used you should normally have the centreboard or daggerboard fully down to keep maximum control and limit sideways drift.

In keelboats there is much more momentum so any stopping manoeuvre requires more time. Anticipation and good crew work are required to slow the boat successfully. Remember that because it is more difficult to do it presents an even bigger opportunity since your opponent may not be able to match your skill.

1.6.2.3 Boat positioning – the control zone

For good boat positioning you should understand the control zone. This is a shared imaginary zone between two boats. When the 'controlling' boat is in the zone its helmsman is able to restrict the other boat's ability to manoeuvre. The commonest situation is being astern or overlapped on one side from where you can stop a boat tacking or gybing.

Generally the bigger and heavier the boat or the more windy the conditions the bigger the control zone. This is because the room a boat needs to carry out a manoeuvre will increase with the size and, generally speaking, the speed of the boats. Diagram 1.19 shows how the zone extends for a typical dinghy when another boat sits on her windward quarter to stop her tacking. The zones are smaller when the leading boat has to gybe since if done correctly a gybe is a very quick manoeuvre. The zones are also slightly bigger if the boat has to tack onto port, since they cannot force the other boat to tack, but are instead going to need room to duck the approaching starboard boat.

Wilson 2000 – USA in blue Nº 5 & 6. On a beat, Nº 5 flaps her jib and heels to windward to slow opposition boats (Nº 1 & Nº 2, the boat astern of Nº 6) by casting windshadow

As a result USA 6 is able to sail higher and faster than the other boats and soon pops out in front. Yellow 1 & 2 must now contemplate tacking off to clear their wind. They should have done this some time ago. Blue (USA) has now achieved a stable position with 5 & 6 in a strong 1st & 2nd

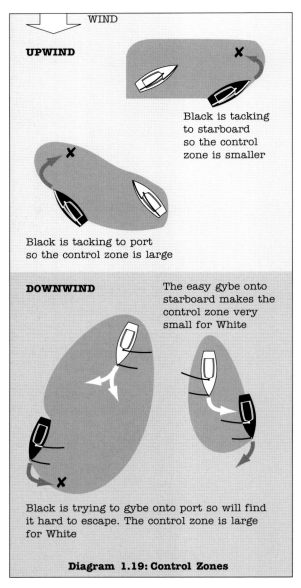

Diagram 1.19: Control Zones

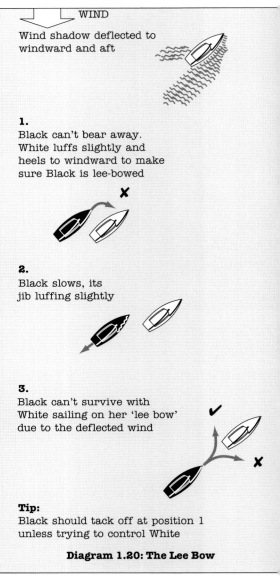

Diagram 1.20: The Lee Bow

- ○ If the escape manoeuvre is quick, the control zone is smaller (e.g., a Firefly tacking).
- ○ If the escape manoeuvre is difficult and slow, the control zone is large (light winds, keelboats).
- ○ If escape involves tacking or gybing onto starboard the control zone is smaller as you gain right-of-way.
- ○ If turning onto port the control zone is larger as you become give-way boat.

To get into the control zone requires some guile since the other boat will see you coming and want to get out of the way. First of all try to make your situation easier by catching them when they are on starboard so their escape would have to be onto the give-way tack. The weapon of surprise is important here. Many of the manoeuvres in Part II rely on getting into the control zone as a major part of executing the manoeuvre. Understanding it, finding it and staying in it are the key to many scenarios.

1.6.2.4 The Lee Bow Position – *Diagram 1.20*
This is a skill which combines both windshadow control and boat positioning in a specific way. It is fundamental to many manoeuvres.

In order to maximise the lee bow wind shadow effect the leeward boat (White in Diagram 1.20) can:

Wilson Trophy 2001 – Rob Sherrington (Nº24) squeezes the author (crewed by Sally Cuthbert) to windward. Richard Guy the crew of 24 watches what's happening so Rob can look forward

- Sheet the sails in hard. Hooking the mainsail leech causes the wind to be even more deflected and turbulent.
- Heel the boat to windward. Bringing the rigs of the two boats closer together again increases the effect. The windward boat should also try and heel to windward to separate the rigs.
- Concentrate on boat positioning as well. The trapped boat needs to be just overlapped, very close to windward. To get up into this position the boat may need to sail very close to the wind and even make a series of luffs. Since the leeward boat initiates and controls the luff she will normally gain. Once the lee bow position is obtained, sail a normal close-hauled course and begin over-sheeting.

It is also possible to carry out the lee bow in keelboats. Use the traveller and mainsheet to hook the mainsail leech. Be careful because the greater weight of a keelboat may mean the boat behind can drive over or under you if you slow too much.

When carrying out a leebow in a dinghy the primary thing to remember is to hike out hard. This will help heel the rig over and allow the mainsail to be oversheeted. It will also mean that your bodies become a bigger obstruction for the give-way windward boat to avoid if he is close to you.

1.6.2.5 Tacking out – Diagram 1.21

It is useful to be able to tack the boat through an abnormal arc. A sharper turn or "over-rotation" quickly brings the boat around onto a close reach. This can be a very useful way of tacking and ducking another boat when the alternative would be to remain trapped (see also Diagram 4.3).

The key skill here is to assess the arc that the bow of your boat will swing through as you turn. If it hits the leeward quarter of the windward boat which is covering, then you got it wrong! You can learn to judge this more accurately by asking your practice partner to tell you how much you miss him by as you do a practice tacking duel. Being able to tack out well makes it harder for an opponent to get into your control zone. This tack out option is made even more feasible by developing the ability to over-rotate in a tack so that you turn further than normal to clear the other boat's transom. Rotating sharply with a vigorous tiller movement, deliberately out of sympathy with the speed of the boat, will cause the boat to slow and thus allow you to drop back a bit and find tacking out safer (although slow).

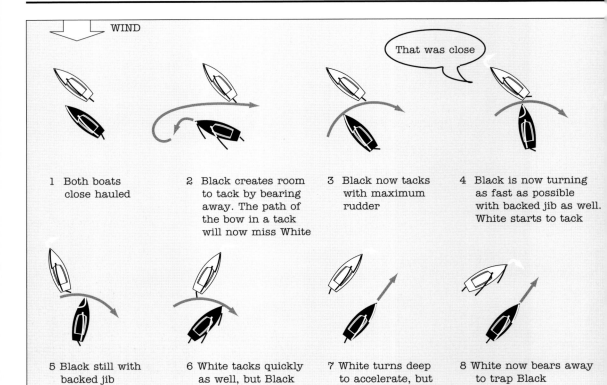

1 Both boats close hauled

2 Black creates room to tack by bearing away. The path of the bow in a tack will now miss White

3 Black now tacks with maximum rudder

4 Black is now turning as fast as possible with backed jib as well. White starts to tack

5 Black still with backed jib

6 White tacks quickly as well, but Black has sailed deep to reaccelerate

7 White turns deep to accelerate, but Black is now fast

8 White now bears away to trap Black

Note:
At 2, White could bear away as well to prevent Black tacking

At 6, Black has now gained luffing rights due to the overlap created by White's tack (Rule 17.1, On the Same Tack: Proper Course – last sentence)

Diagram 1.21: Tacking out of a gap

1.6.2.6 Penalty turns

Doing a three-sixty degree or seven-twenty degree penalty turn requires a combination of efficient roll gybing and tacking. There are a number of things to remember to make the turn or turns faster.

❍ It is normally best to start the turn with a gybe. This often proves quicker since the gybe is easier while the boat is still moving fast and the momentum of the main coming across aids the rest of your turn. Obviously if another boat obstructs your gybing route start with a tack.

❍ Time your sail trimming and turn so that they are in sympathy and as quick as possible. Sail the boat round; don't force it with excessive rudder angles. It is normally best not to let go of either tiller or sheet since the subsequent loss of control will take longer to put right.

❍ The helm and crew should use their weight to heel the boat to assist the turn. Rudderless sailing will help to highlight how effective this can be.

❍ The crew should move swiftly across the boat and may help the boom come across early in the gybe by pulling on the kicker (vang) or boom.

❍ The plate should be down and the kicker tensioned slightly and mainsail partially sheeted in ahead of the gybe.

Remember that you may need to sail clear of all other boats to start your turn and that the umpires will be expecting you to do this promptly. If you fail to keep clear during your turns and therefore delay part of them for a length of time, that may be considered an invalid circle. If the opposition then protest further you may have additional turns to do(Rule 20, **Penalty Turns**).

1.6.2.7 Sailing the groove

This skill refers to the ability of a helm and crew to sail a high or low close hauled course while still making good ground to windward. By sailing high and pinching up they maximise the height gained to windward, at least in the short term. When sailing low they are accelerated to maximum speed and therefore pull forward on a normal beating boat but lose some height to windward.

The key skill points are:

Sailing high
○ sails flatter
○ pinching course
○ weight forward
○ boat level; hike hard

Sailing low and fast
○ sails with some twist and eased slightly
○ trim for maximum speed
○ boat level
○ use gusts and waves to drive off

Tip: Hike hard – it works!

1.6.2.8 Individual starting skills

The tactics and skills of starting as a **team** are looked at in Part II. In this section we examine some additional individual skills which make for successful starting.

Being on the line...

The ability to be on the line, at the desired spot at speed when the start signal goes can be broken down into a number of key areas:

○ Having an excellent countdown to the start.
○ Judging accurately your distance from the line.
○ Accelerating and decelerating the boat in a controlled way.
○ Being able to avoid stalling the boat when stopped.
○ Judging the position of your last turn towards the line such that you can start on time.
○ Not letting other boats disturb your ability to arrive at the line on time.

All of these skills can be practised individually or in small groups by doing repeated starting, say every two minutes. A good sailing coach will be able to help develop the relevant skills.

Layline identification

The start line has laylines to both ends as shown in Diagram 1.22. You need to be continually aware of these when starting and must be able to line up below, above or on them as your starting strategy requires. If you find yourself too low on a layline the skill is to climb up to it by a series of luffs. Alternatively, if above one you

may be able to "lose height" and drift, or dive down on to the layline, but only if your opponents allow you to.

As a team racer you can measure your starting skill yourself by starting on either side of a mark every two minutes. Having started you immediately go back and try again. Devise a scoring system, or measure of success, so you can gauge your improvement, so that you are always able to be within a metre of the buoy each time. In addition, try and arrange team starting practices with an observer watching the line accurately and letting team members know the distance under/over the line at each go.

1.6.3 Dealing with the Rules

1.6.3.1 Understanding the structure of the Rules

The rules concerned with 'when boats meet on the course' are logically divided up into:

1. Rules 10 to 13 which create a "right-of-way" boat and a "keep-clear" or "give-way" boat.
2. Additional "General Limitations" and "Other Rules" which are additional obligations which may apply in particular circumstances. These are detailed in Rules 14 to 22 and may modify a scenario by placing additional requirements on a boat. Appendix D also carries a few additional general limitations or modifications to them specifically for team racing.
3. Rule 18.2, **Giving Room; Keeping Clear**, Rule 18.3, **Tacking at a Mark**, Rule 18.5, **Passing a Continuing Obstruction** and Rule 20, **Starting Errors; Penalty Turns; Moving Astern** are exceptional in that their application to a scenario effectively overrides Rules 10 to 13 and the right-of-way boat is determined by the application of the specific rule. In this respect these rules create a right-of-way boat and a keep-clear boat just as in 1 above, if they are relevant to the incident.

Right-of-Way boat is determined by application of:

Rule 10	On Opposite Tacks
Rule 11	On the Same Tack, Overlapped
Rule 12	On The Same Tack, Not Overlapped
Rule 13	While Tacking

or

Right-of-Way may be created by application of:

Rule 18.2	Giving Room; Keeping Clear
Rule 18.3	Tacking at a Mark
Rule 18.5	Passing a Continuing Obstruction
Rule 20	Starting Errors; Penalty Turns; Moving Astern

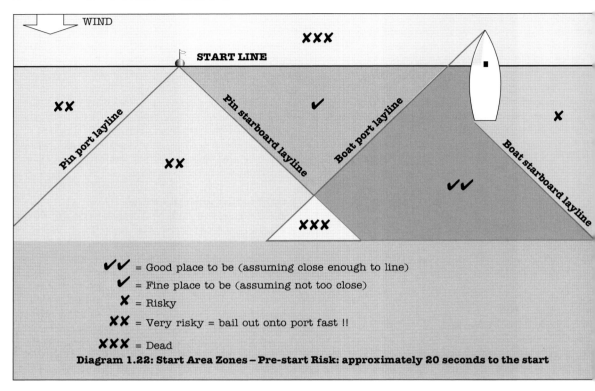

Diagram 1.22: Start Area Zones – Pre-start Risk: approximately 20 seconds to the start

plus

Additional obligations are applied by:

Rule 14	Avoiding Contact
Rule 15	Acquiring Right-of-Way
Rule 16	Changing Course
Rule 17	On the Same Tack; Proper Course
Rule 18	Rounding and Passing Marks and Obstructions
Rule 19	Room to Tack at an Obstruction
Rule 21	Capsized, Anchored or Aground; Rescuing
Rule 22	Interfering with Another Boat
Appendix D	Team Racing Rules

Note: Certain key words shown in The Rule Book in italics are explained in the section of the Rule Book entitled Definitions.

Important Definitions to understand are:
❏ Clear Astern and Clear Ahead
❏ Overlap
❏ Keep Clear
❏ Proper Course
❏ Room

The responsibilities on each boat are defined

A boat may therefore breach the rules in two fundamental ways:
1. It may fail to Keep Clear of a Right-of-Way boat.
2. It may fail to satisfy one of the obligations applicable to the scenario.

Top Tip: In any given scenario aim to know:

1. **Who has Right-of-Way**
2. **What are the obligations on each of the boats involved**

The Rules in Practice by Bryan Willis (also published by Fernhurst Books) is specifically structured to this approach

---

1.6.3.2 The incident process:
1. A boat becomes "right-of-way boat".
2. A right-of-way boat attains (through their action or the give-way boat's action) a collision course.
3. A collision either occurs or one or both boats take avoiding action.

Rights gained → Collision course →
Avoidance or collision – Who is right?

After this sequence of events the competitors and umpires (if they are there) are left wondering who is right. To understand how to interpret the events look at Rules 14, 15 and 16. These important general limitations are relevant to so many manoeuvres that they are really the "**Global Rules**" which you need to understand for every scenario.

Rule 14, **Avoiding Contact** basically means it is possible that you may be disqualified if, as right-of-way boat, you contribute to the damage in a collision. It is most likely that a competitor's involvement with this Rule would take the form of an after-race hearing and possible penalty.

Rule 15, **Acquiring Right of Way** states that when a boat acquires right of way, she shall initially give the other boat room to keep clear, unless she acquires right-of-way because of the other boat's actions. This rule means there is a burden on a boat as she becomes right-of-way which requires her to allow the other boat time to respond. This means you need to be conscious of the moment when you become right-of-way. It may be advisable to communicate this to your opponent (e.g., by hailing "overlapped") so that they and the umpires are clear on the situation.

Once you have gained right-of-way it may be that either:

❍ the other boat is not on a collision course with you, or
❍ the other boat is far enough away from you that there is no immediate risk of a collision.

In these situations you may want to attempt to obstruct, control, or attempt to pass on a penalty to your opponent by making the situation much closer. You are therefore interested in changing course towards the other boat such that there is an increasing risk of collision.

As you alter course towards a give-way boat you are subject to…

Rule 16, **Changing Course** which states, when a right-of-way boat changes course, she shall give the other boat room to keep clear. This means that there is a continued burden on the right-of-way boat. This burden is defined by "Room" and "Keep Clear".

Room is the space a boat needs in the existing conditions while manoeuvring promptly in a seamanlike way.

Keep Clear… One boat keeps clear of another if the other can sail her course with no need to take avoiding action and, when the boats are overlapped on the same tack, if the leeward boat could change course in both directions without immediately making contact with the windward boat (see Diagram 1.23).

This basically means that the give-way boat can respond reasonably steadily as long as it is prompt. This is sufficient response to any alteration by the right-of-way boat. The give-way boat is never expected to have to act in panic in an unseamanlike way.

If at any moment the straight line course of a right-of-way boat means there is no collision course then a give-way boat can momentarily relax since if the right-of-way boat alters they become burdened by Rule 16. If the boats are on the same tack then if they are close the windward boat should start to move away before they get so close that a collision is an immediate risk.

Rule 16.2, **Changing Course**, has an additional condition involving boats which are crossing one another (a common occurrence in team racing). It means that if a port tack boat is safely crossing ahead or ducking behind a starboard boat, the right-of-way starboard boat should not change course when the boats are close. This rule is aimed at restricting the right-of-way boat 'hunting' the give-way boat. It does not apply during the pre-start time. Usually when boats are on a run the starboard boat can make it clear that the port boat cannot cross due to the presence of the starboard boat. The effect of this is that hunting does happen on the run. On the beat crossing is more likely and effectively you cannot hunt successfully on the beat (Diagram 1.24).

Nothing in the rules says you cannot slow down or heel the boat to make the keep-clear boat find things more difficult.

1.6.3.3 Transitions

Any boat should always be conscious of the transitions which are taking place on the water. By a transition I mean a change in "right of way/give way" or a change in the "general limitations" on a boat. For example:

Change in right-of-way:
❍ Gaining right of way by:
  ❑ changing tack onto starboard
  ❑ tacking or gybing into a leeward overlap
  ❑ gaining a leeward overlap from behind
❍ Going through head to wind
❍ Starting/completing a return to the start having been "on course side"
❍ Completing penalty turns
❍ Starting to move astern (or starting to go forwards again)
❍ Getting to a close-hauled course after passing through head-to-wind (this is important for Rule 13), or

Obligations created by:
❍ Starting to alter course
❍ Stopping altering course

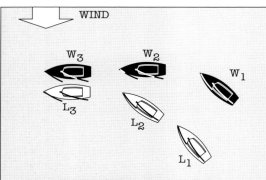

RULE 11 – On the Same Tack, Overlapped
Source: Team Racing Call Book

QUESTION:
L and W are both on starboard tack sailing to windward. W bears off to "sit on" L. L bears away to gybe out but W gets so close that L is unable to point up or bear away without immediately colliding with W. L protests and displays her yellow flag. What should the call be?

ANSWER:
The definition of KEEPING CLEAR requires that the leeward boat can change course without immediately making contact with the windward boat. W as windward boat has not kept clear and has infringed Rule 11 – On the Same Tack, Overlapped. Penalise W (windward, too close)

Diagram 1.23: On the Same Tack, Overlapped

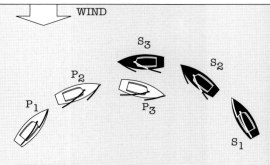

RULE: 16.2

QUESTION:
P and S are on a beat. P bears off to pass astern of S, S then bears off but does not prevent P from keeping clear. P protests and displays her yellow flag.
What should the call be ?

ANSWER:
P is give-way and is "crossing" (ducking is crossing as well). S breaks Rule 16.2, Changing Course, because her change of course (at S_2) requires an **immediate** change of course by P for it to continue to keep clear.
Penalise S – Hunting

NOTE, this is different from Fleet and Match racing

Diagram 1.24: Hunting

○ Starting to respond
○ Entering the two length zone of a mark (Rule 18) or of a same tack boat (Rule 17)
○ Finishing
○ Becoming "about to pass a mark"
○ Completing "passing a mark"
○ Masthead touching water (Rule 21)
○ Reaching the point where a collision is inevitable unless the right-of-way boat alters course. The list could go on…

It is important that you identify these transitions and any change in **responsibility** for a boat. The transition will be the moment where a boat either comes under **threat** from its (now) better placed opponent or where the threat has now **ended**. It may represent a new subset of rules now becoming relevant to the scenario. Often the transition will result in a change in who has right of way and so Rules 14, 15 and 16 will apply with 16, **Changing Course**, in particular being the rule which then controls the **rate of change** of the situation.

Deciding what and when transitions occur is the main technique used by umpires. As a competitor it is important that you try to understand the transitions thoroughly.

If you are ever trying to understand a tactical rule situation for a protest, examine first the transitions which took place, find out if they are agreed and most importantly establish the sequence in which they occurred.

When reading the manoeuvre chapters it is important to note the transitions which are particularly relevant to each scenario. Refer back to the rules as you read.

1.6.3.4 Racing when Umpired
To try and overcome the considerable complexity of rules scenarios, the umpires and competitors have worked together to produce a **Call Book**. This outlines some of the more "transitional" tactical scenarios and gives an agreed interpretation which may be the one the umpire will agree on. This book is available from the UK Team Racing Association and ISAF. While it is primarily intended as a technical manual for umpires

Wilson 2000 – Mark time fun. N°25 & 29 need to be clear on their rights. Did 25 have room? Will 29 avoid a dangerous collision? (In fact both boats got around OK!) 27 & 28 also look to be set up for a very close shave! The Jury boat watches from astern and is probably a bit worried – can they see what's happening?

you may find it a useful additional guide.

> Umpires use a fundamental rule for helping them decide what has happened. It is:
> **If I am uncertain, I will go back to the last time I was certain**

For example, if a boat is passing through head to wind, which in the rules is an instantaneous moment, the umpire will not say that a boat is tacking until they are **certain** the boat is no longer on the old tack. Similarly if you are trying to get an overlap on a boat ahead of you the umpire will assume that no overlap exists until he is **certain** it does. You are well advised to do the same thing and always be cautious when you pass through a transition to a right-of-way situation and allow the umpire **time to be sure** that this has happened (Diagram 1.25).

The umpiring process works in the same way as a portable protest committee. This means that, in most circumstances, the umpire does not initiate action against competitors unless the competitors themselves **request** it. The competitors are expected to try and establish voluntarily if either of them is to blame for an incident prior to the involvement of the umpire. This

means that the following sequence is followed:

1. An incident occurs.
2. One, or both, boats hail "protest" loudly, and display a **red flag**. This signal should be audible and visible to both the other competitor and the nearby umpire.
3. A period of response time is allowed.
4. The purpose of this "reasonable time" of probably 5 to 10 seconds is that one or both boats may choose to do a voluntary 360° turn, **or**
5. One or both boats may now decide to involve the umpires by clearly raising a **yellow flag** and hailing "Umpire".
6. The umpire now has a period for thought and may take some time to respond.
7. The umpire makes a decision which is indicated by a coloured flag accompanied by a loud whistle and/or hail to draw attention to it. The flag will be pointed at the boat it applies to. The flags used and their meanings are as follows:
   - ❏ **Green** = no penalty imposed, incident closed
   - ❏ **Red** pointed at one or more boats = penalty awarded (normally a 720° turn)
   - ❏ **Black** = the boat indicated may be required to attend an umpire-initiated post-race

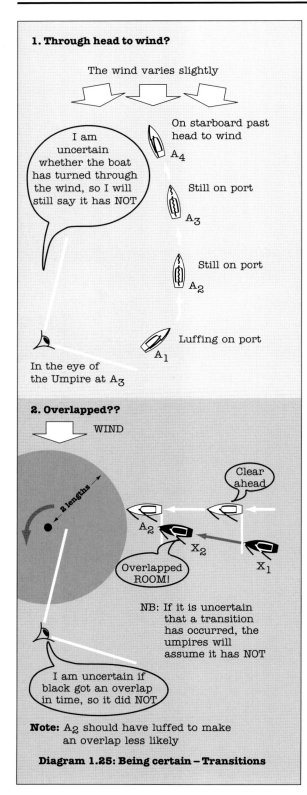

Diagram 1.25: Being certain – Transitions

hearing which will consider matters such as 'reckless sailing' or 'failing to comply with a decision'.

8.   Any penalised boat now has a short time to sail clear and start doing turns.

A competitor may choose to do a voluntary 360° turn as late as stage 6. However, if the umpire considers that the turn followed the incident too slowly, he may well then demand a 720° turn. By doing a voluntary turn too late (i.e., after you have raised your yellow flag), you could well end up having to do both a voluntary 360° turn **plus** an umpire imposed 720° spin.

> **Reasons for a Green Flag to be flown:**
>
> 1.   **No incident, i.e., no Rule was broken**
>
> 2.   **The Umpire was unsighted**
>
> 3.   **The decision was too complex, the Umpires disagree or believe that both boats have some blame**
>
> 4.   **The correct protest procedure was not carried out, i.e. it was an invalid protest (e.g., Yellow flag flown too soon after Red)**

If a boat is still considered to have gained by a foul, despite carrying out either a voluntary turn or an imposed 720° turn, then their opposition should protest again. It is possible, particularly if the umpire feels that it was a "professional" attempt to gain by breaking a rule, that an additional penalty may be awarded. An umpire may also have to respond to a protest from one of the teams that their opponents have not carried out a penalty in a reasonable time. If the umpire finds that this is the case an additional penalty will be imposed.

In the event that additional penalty turns are awarded, the Red Flag is again waved, and the umpire will normally hail how many turns he now expects the competitor to make. For example, "four turns required" because the first penalty was not carried out.

In the 1995 UK selection trial, Russell Peters was awarded four turns in the final race. Russell had been given two turns, disagreed, then delayed and "discussed" the decision with the umpire. The result was conclusive for the race – Russell went from 2nd to 6th.

The Black Flag can also be used to allow the option of bringing the result ashore if additional turns for the penalised boat cannot bring justice.

Observing
Observing is a simpler, less labour-intensive type of

SUMMARY OF KEY SKILLS FEATURES

HOW WILL YOU DO?

YOUR SKILLS
- Are you well practiced as a team and as individuals?
- Is your rules knowledge good?

THEIR SKILLS
- Are the opposition fast?
- Are they well practised as a team?
- What skill gaps exist in their team?
- Do they have good rules knowledge?

BOAT TYPE
- Is the boat manoeuvrable?
- Does the boat stop and accelerate quickly?
- Does it stall quickly when stopped?
- Does it have a wide "groove"?
  - (point high & foot off well)
- What characteristics does the windshadow have?
- Is there variation between boats – is the boat the same as everyone else's?
  - (e.g., tuning, weed, sails?)

CONDITIONS
- Is it windy enough to be risky for certain manoeuvres?
- Is it light – will it be difficult to control the boat in sharp manoeuvres?
- How shifty are the conditions?
  - (relevant for balance and leverage)
- How gusty or patchy is the wind?
- Is there a wave or boat wake problem?
  - (Due to Umpires, traffic, wave refraction)

race policing which means that fewer judges are needed to watch the race. They can, therefore, "observe" more races at the same time for the same umpiring resource. This method has the advantage that observers may leave and join the race at any time. The observing option means that umpires' time will not be wasted on races with no incidents, but it has the disadvantage that some incidents may be missed.

As under the umpiring system, the same penalty turn and flag system are used, however, there is an additional option for the observer involving the Yellow Flag. Flying a Yellow Flag means that the observer will not make a decision immediately, possibly because he was unsighted. It leaves open the option of taking a protest ashore. Note that the protesting boat will have

to comply with the protest procedure (Rule 61) in order for a protest to occur. The Yellow Flag is viewed as an unpopular option by most competitors and observers since protest hearings, particularly when there are no reliable witnesses, may not always end in a fair result. Nevertheless, if a collision has occurred, and if an observer knows that just a few questions to the competitors will resolve the issue, the Yellow Flag may be the correct route to follow. Alternatively, the observer can choose to ask questions while the race continues and then decide whether or not to fly a Yellow Flag.

Tip: When intending to do a voluntary 360° turn make this clear by telling your opponent and the Umpire of your intention.

PART II
TEAM RACING MANOEUVRES

In this section we will look around the racecourse at the various team racing manoeuvres. When team racing they are the bread and butter of changing the way the race is going for your team. When fleet racing understanding these manoeuvres will help your rapid progress round the course, defending your position, avoiding risks and giving you the skill to position your boat well in all close situations. Through skillful management of a situation you can optimise the chance of getting an advantage.

In each scenario we'll identify and examine the key points:

> Which boat has the best **position** for attacking/defending?
> What is the best **action** for:
   ❏ Attacking?
   ❏ Defending?
> What are the **risks** for the different boats?
> What are the **key skills** highlighted in the manoeuvre?
> What are the main rule points highlighted and **"transitions"** that the boats go through in terms of defining who has right of way and what Additional Limitations, Other Rules or aspects of Appendix D (Team Race Rules) place obligations on the boats?

This series of Chapters will enable you to:

> **Know the Options**

> **Appreciate the Obligations**

> **Spot the Opportunities**

You should have read the racing rules, particularly the sections on **When Boats Meet**, the **Team Racing Appendix** and **Definitions**. You should also keep these handy so you can read the relevant sections. This rule knowledge and understanding of the tactical application of the Rules will give a huge advantage for ALL the sailboat racing you may do – team, match or fleet, from club racing to **Olympic medal critical races**.

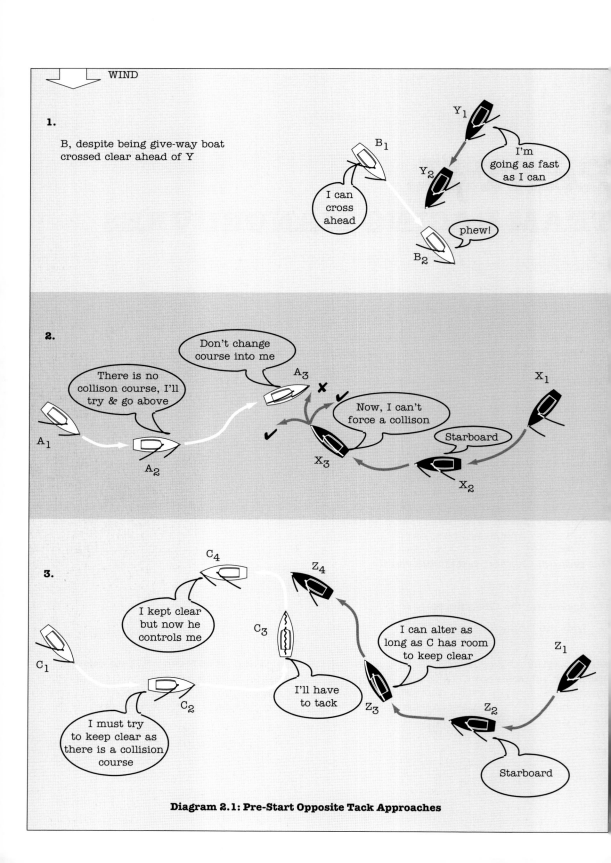

Diagram 2.1: Pre-Start Opposite Tack Approaches

2
PRE-START MANOEUVRES

2.1 BASIC PRE-START

The essential objectives of manoeuvring pre-start are:

1. **To get the best possible individual and team starts**
2. **To prevent your opposition from getting good starts**

While it isn't necessary for you to go on the offensive and get closely involved with your opponents they might choose to come and try and control you so you need to be aware of the normal close-quarter "match race" style tactics.

2.1.1 Controlling and escaping

The skills of "control zoning" are used to try and restrict the ability of a boat ahead to manoeuvre freely. In this context the boat astern is the attacker and the boat ahead, who may have difficulty tacking, gybing or bearing away, is the defender. It is like shepherd and sheep once one boat gets astern of another, so during the pre-start boats try and avoid getting caught and watch for opportunities to drop in behind opponents and control them.

Assuming that the boats initially come together from opposite tacks neither will be clearly ahead or astern. In this situation the starboard tack boat is the 'hunter' and will be aiming to force the port tack boat to turn and run away and hence be controlled. The port tack boat is simply trying to get away without being controlled. As the two boats come together the starboard boat has the right to alter course but is restricted by Rule 16, **Changing Course**. The port boat may then have some options but depending on the positioning, course and speed of the starboard boat it may be forced into a particular action. The options the port boat has are as follows, in order of preference (Diagram 2.1):

1. Cross ahead of the starboard boat thus getting to leeward of it and remaining on port.
2. Pass to windward of the starboard boat and remain on port.
3. Tack or gybe onto starboard.

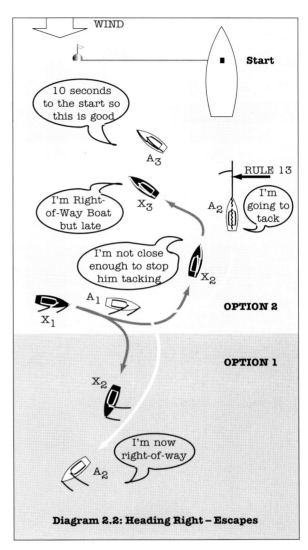

Diagram 2.2: Heading Right – Escapes

The port boat must remember to act promptly once the starboard boat is on a collision course. As long as there is no collision course the port boat need not respond.

After they have got close it is likely that one boat will turn by tacking or gybing to attempt to get astern of the other. For example in Diagram 2.1, after X_3, X might choose to tack and chase A. A can respond by either:

1. Sailing on as fast as possible,
2. Tacking or gybing in response, thereby starting to turn in the same direction as the other boat.

If adopting the first method the boat will either be confident of being able to escape later, for example by gybing onto starboard, or will be heading to the start line. In the second instance, if a turn has been used

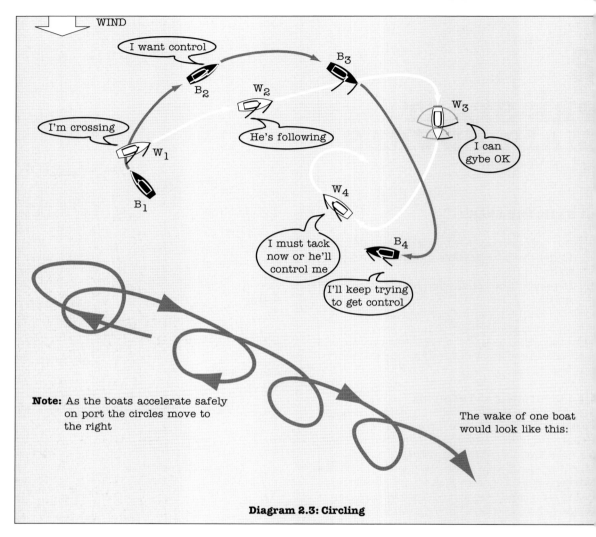

Diagram 2.3: Circling

then the two boats are likely to start "circling" in a tail-chasing manoeuvre where each is seeking to get the other into a control zone (Diagram 2.3).

If one boat gets the advantage then they will either be heading off on port or starboard.

2.1.2 Heading right

If heading off on port the lead boat has several escape options and so the tailing boat will have to be quite close if they are going to keep the pair moving off to the right. The lead boat could try and do the following to try and shake off the pursuer (in increasing order of difficulty):
1. Gybe onto starboard
2. Tack onto starboard

The gybe is easier to do because the boat instantly achieves the full status of a starboard boat, but as is the case in Diagram 2.2 you need to be sure you are not

going too far from the line. A tacking boat, however, has to get through to closehauled before it is clearly not going to contravene Rule 13, **While Tacking**.

> **Tip: It is normally possible to escape by gybing onto starboard**

2.1.3 Heading left – Diagrams 2.4, 2.5 & 2.6
In the other direction any change of tack by the leading boat will result in its finishing on port. Inevitably this means that the controlled boat must use more cunning to get away. It is worth trying a sharp luff, bearing away or slowing down, as long as none of these options has much risk of fouling the other boat. Fouling is a danger if the other boat goes to leeward and becomes right of way. If the tailing boat gets too far to leeward the tack is a good option. It is best to get out of being tailed off to the left as soon as possible.

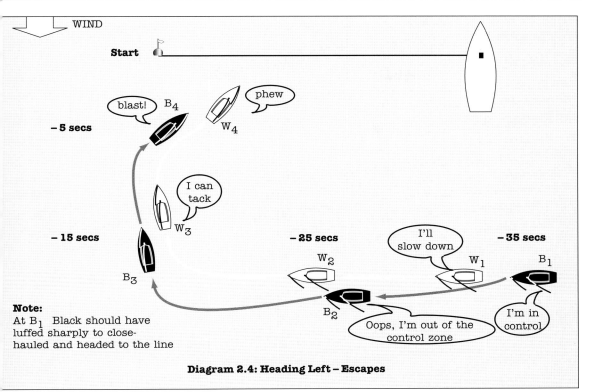

Diagram 2.4: Heading Left – Escapes

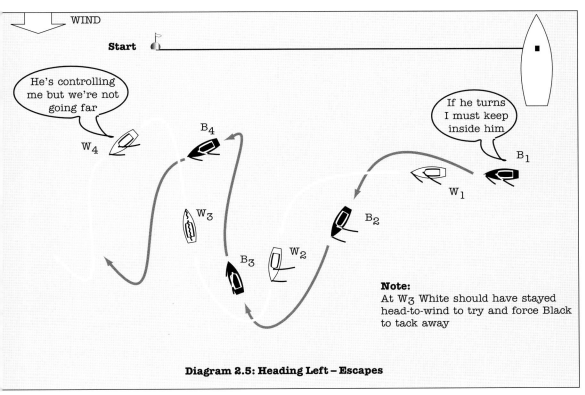

Diagram 2.5: Heading Left – Escapes

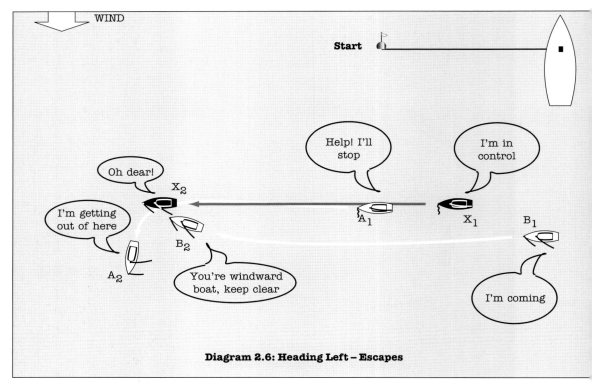

Diagram 2.6: Heading Left – Escapes

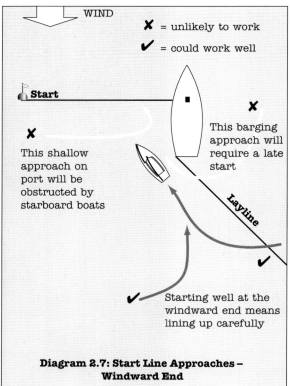

Diagram 2.7: Start Line Approaches – Windward End

The tailing boat should concentrate on matching the speed of the other boat so she does not overhaul her and leave open the option of a tack or gybe. The tailing boat should also always try to turn inside the lead boat so as to remain in a position to prevent the other boat circling.

If all else fails the boat being tailed to the left should not go too far from the line. She should slow, for example by luffing to head to wind, and await or even ask for the help of a team mate. The team mate should come in to leeward of the tailing boat, therefore acquiring rights as leeward boat. The originally trapped boat is now free to gybe out onto port, leaving her team mate in control of the situation.

> **Tip:** It is bad to be chased left, do not go far if trapped, luff up and stop

2.2 ADVANCED PRE-START

If one of the opposition team is particularly strong then you may want to maximise the chances of neutralising them before the start. An effective way of doing this can be to dedicate two team members to work together on that boat. Two on one is always more likely to result in the opposition boat being controlled.

Winning sailors will be aware of where on the line

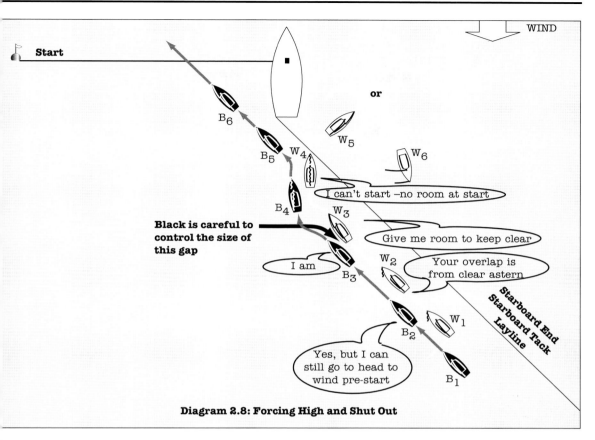

Diagram 2.8: Forcing High and Shut Out

they would like to start but will give overriding importance to the location of other boats. They will therefore be flexible. In particular, when lining up prior to the start signal, they will be looking for defensive and offensive opportunities:

Defensive:

. Ensure space to leeward, to free off into for speed, or to turn into if early.

?. Beware an enemy boat overlapped "instantaneously" to leeward; he will be able to luff above close hauled.

3. Beware windward boats creating windshadow.

Offensive:

. Position close enough to windward boats to leebow them after the start.

?. Attempt to secure luffing rights on any windward boat.

3. Be prepared to force enemy boats 'On Course Side' or late.

4. Use windshadow to blanket opponents to slow them or make them late.

Ideally boats should line up so that they have freedom to tack. Ideally boats should line up so as to restrict any escape options for opposition boats. Diagram 2.7 highlights the possible successful ways of approaching the start for a windward end.

2.2.1 Tailing in, Forcing high
Chasing a boat ahead of you in the pre-start and going to leeward of them, pushing them up to windward.

Now we need to gain an understanding of how the rules and definitions interact to influence the pre-start luff. Rule 17, **On The Same Tack; Proper Course**, and in particular Rule 17.1 allows the leeward, right-of-way boat to come up to its proper course having established an overlap on another boat and expect the windward boat to comply with Rule 11, **On The Same Tack; Overlapped**. The interesting point here is that "proper course" is defined BUT the definition says "A boat has no proper course before her starting signal". This means that a pre-start leeward boat can expect to come up to head-to-wind, regardless of how the boats became overlapped, as long as it allows the windward boat room to keep clear. Room to keep clear might well include expecting the windward boat to continue

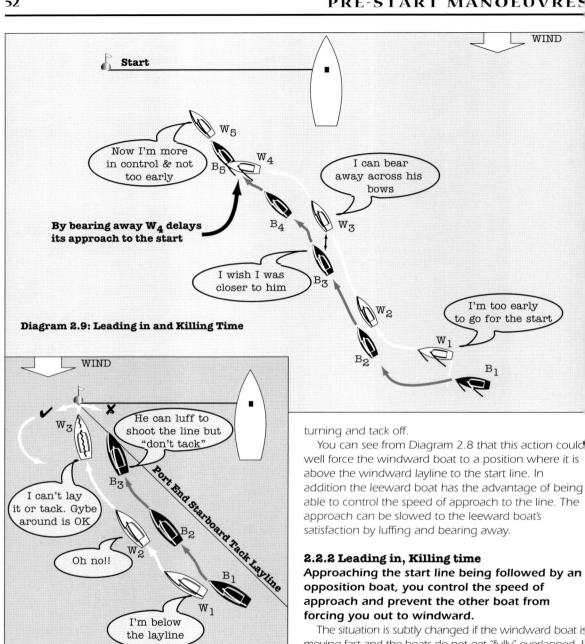

Diagram 2.9: Leading in and Killing Time

Diagram 2.10: Port End Shut Out

Note: Better for W, at position 2 to have sailed faster earlier so as to bear away, tack and then start sailing fast on port. If White's team-mates control the windward end, White will emerge uncovered with a good position on the right hand side of the course

turning and tack off.

You can see from Diagram 2.8 that this action could well force the windward boat to a position where it is above the windward layline to the start line. In addition the leeward boat has the advantage of being able to control the speed of approach to the line. The approach can be slowed to the leeward boat's satisfaction by luffing and bearing away.

2.2.2 Leading in, Killing time
Approaching the start line being followed by an opposition boat, you control the speed of approach and prevent the other boat from forcing you out to windward.

The situation is subtly changed if the windward boat is moving fast and the boats do not get "fully" overlapped. If the leeward boat comes in to gain a leeward overlap from clear astern she is constrained by Rule 15, **Acquiring Right of Way** and initially has to give the windward boat room to keep clear. This slight delay in response is a boost to the leading boat's options: she can probably manage to harden up to close hauled. In doing so she will blanket the trailing leeward boat who will also not be able to accelerate as quickly. It is likely the overlap will be broken, therefore giving the leading boat right of way. The leading boat can now bear away across the

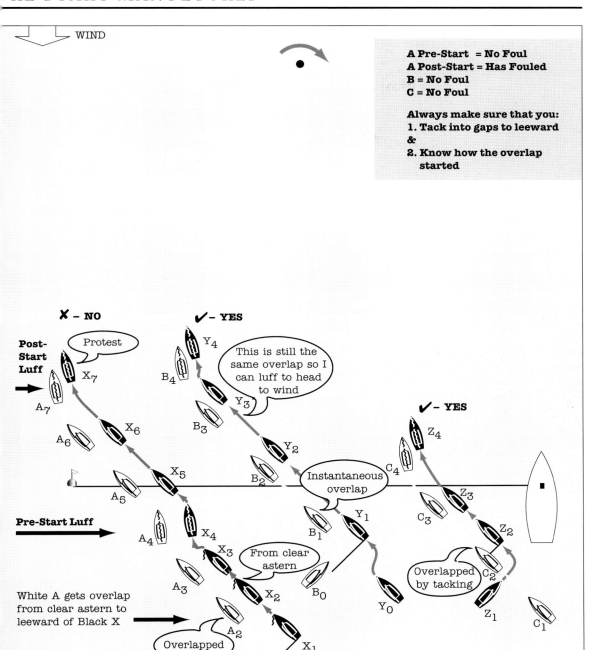

Diagram 2.11: Pre-Start Overlaps

bow of the tailing give-way boat, and until a new overlap is established it can use this bearing away manoeuvre to delay its approach to the line. A series of bear away, luff, accelerate, break overlap, bear away can continue all the way to the line with the lead boat arriving on time and the tailing boat late.

This manoeuvre will only work if the windward/clear ahead boat has sufficient speed and room to be able to control the overlap situation. During the manoeuvre (in Diagram 2.9) you can see both boats lose ground away from the windward layline. Black is at risk of not laying the line at all. Once Black realises they are very late they will probably start tacking to try and break the cover and clear their air.

2.2.3 Force out at either end

As the final approach to the line is made we have already pointed out that a boat to windward and near the layline is risking being pushed above it, which would be a critical problem as the boat to windward risks being prevented from having room to start. It is important to remember that even as the start line buoy or committee boat are approached there is no right for room for the windward overlapped boat because Rule 18.1, Rounding and Passing Marks and Obstructions under exception (a) specifically excludes the application of room at a starting mark. So, **no barging** (Diagram 2.8).

In addition there is the opportunity to hold a boat out at the leeward end. This is quite difficult because the leeward boat has right of way and has the right to luff. Despite the fact that it has no room at the start mark the leeward boat does have the right to luff to its proper course. Since the proper course is to get across the start line, provided (as ever) it is possible for the windward boat to keep clear, then it can shoot up to get through the line. The White boat in Diagram 2.10 must be careful not to go beyond head to wind or it would foul under Rule 13, **Tacking** by becoming give-way boat. This "shooting the line" is thus a function of the rule's definition of proper course. The luff is permissible even if the leeward boat came in from behind provided the give-way windward boat **can** keep clear. If White cannot shoot the line then the **'shut out'** has been successful.

If, instead, as the two boats approach the leeward end the trailing boat goes to leeward, then it is possible that the windward leading boat may be pushed over the start prematurely. You are also referred to Diagram 4.7, Sailing to and Using Obstructions.

2.2.4 Establishing Pre-Start Overlaps

The right to luff is a very important weapon for the team racer in the context of slowing down other boats. Ideally if you find yourself as the leeward boat on a beat you would prefer to be able to luff up to head to wind. Once the starting signal has gone,

however, the proper course becomes defined as close hauled. Let us examine Diagram 2.11.

Pair 1 (A & X) – Overlap from astern by White

White is gaining an overlap that does **not** allow it to sail above its proper course. Before the starting signal there is no proper course defined so a luff to head-to-wind, providing room-to-keep-clear is given, is allowed for White (A_4). A and X then start normally having resumed a close hauled course. When A luffs again (A_7) this is on the beat, still under the same overlap. This luff is therefore above a proper course. Because the overlap was from astern it is invalid – A is in the wrong.

Pair 2 (B & Y) – Tack into overlap by White

Here White B sails underneath Black Y and does a lee bow tack (or a tack ahead after which B gets overlapped to windward). This creates an **instantaneous** or immediate overlap. Throughout the existence of this overlap White will retain the right to luff above its proper course; either before or **after** the starting signal.

Pair 3 (C & Z) – Overlap by a boat ahead tacking on top

Here the Black boat Z approaches on the opposite tack to White C. Black crosses and tacks. Since the boats become overlapped whilst Black is tacking (before it reaches close hauled) White has gained an overlap from astern by a boat ahead tacking. Rule 17.1 is used to constrain boats from luffing. In the last sentence of Rule 17.1 (**On the Same Tack; Proper Course**) it states that...

> "This Rule does not apply if the overlap begins while the windward boat is required by Rule 13 (**Tacking**) to keep clear."

This is a convoluted way of saying the leeward boat gets luffing rights. White can therefore luff up to head-to-wind with full rights.

Pre-start top tips:
- Do not sacrifice a good start by match racing an opponent excessively
- Keep an eye out for your team mates who might need your help
- Watch the breeze and line bias even in the last minute
- Do not sit around on starboard, it is easier to escape from port tack by going onto starboard
- Remember that during pre-start you can luff to head to wind regardless of how you became overlapped
- When approaching the line compromise your start slightly if you can destroy an opponents start
- Be happy to circle but break off in time to start well

3

TEAM STARTING MANOEUVRES

3.1 BASIC STARTING

The last manoeuvre you make in the pre-start is the critical link with a successful start. As you line up, your position relative to other boats and timing of approach will be vital. See Diagram 3.1.

3.1.1 Time traps

During the skills section it was pointed out that the judgement of speed versus time remaining and distance to the line are key elements of a good start.

The team racer should always be careful with their own approach to the line and also be conscious of the other boats in the race. If opposition boats are ahead and to windward of you there may be time to push them over the line early. In this situation it is important to make sure the job is done properly even to the extent of risking being over yourself. The boat to leeward who is pushing the boats over the line may well be over and need to duck back but should find it more straightforward to return than her opponents. It may be possible to prevent the opposition returning for some time, which is a useful tactic if you want the race spread out early on, for example if the trapped boat happens to be their fastest boat. See Diagram 3.2.

If you realise that it is impossible for you to start on time, either because you have misjudged your approach or because another boat is pushing you over then it is important to realise this early. With about 15 seconds to go it may still be possible to cross the start line and sail right round the end leaving the opposition boat exposed, sitting there "on course side" as the gun goes (Diagram 3.3).

In order to play the time tactics to your team's advantage it is worth considering **not** all lining up at the same time. Lining up early cuts down your flexibility and therefore will give a tactical advantage to an opponent. The length of the line in relationship to

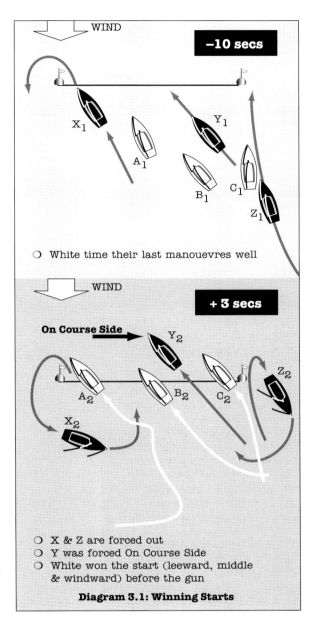

○ White time their last manoeuvres well

On Course Side

○ X & Z are forced out
○ Y was forced On Course Side
○ White won the start (leeward, middle & windward) before the gun

Diagram 3.1: Winning Starts

the size and number of boats is an important variable. If the line is short make sure you can get on it. If the line is long you can afford to make a late approach into a gap and hence choose how close you want to be to other boats.

3.1.2 Being in a particular place on the line – location logic

Where to start on the line is not as important as being ahead of your opposition and going faster, but is still worth thinking about. The element of line bias may

Worlds – GBR 2 are in grey with 4 seconds to the start (N° 16, 17 & 18). Note how close the boats are to the line
  N°18, Richard Robinson, is approaching late but at speed. He may be in time to force 13 to sail over the line
  and then win the leeward end. N°13 must luff up and sail forward because she is windward boat

mean it is particularly important to win a certain end
since this boat or boats will have an immediate
advantage in the race due to being further upwind.
The short length of team race start lines normally make
this advantage minimal. The location of a boat on a
line, even a line perfectly square to the wind, still has
some important tactical considerations.

3.1.2.1 Winning the ends
'Winning the end' means that you have started closest
to your preferred end of the line and are well placed,
in fact in a dominating position, relative to any
opposition boats near you. It does not necessarily
mean you have to be at the end, just that you are
closer to the end than the others. In a congested fleet
race it rarely pays to risk trying to win an end of the
start line. In team racing there are only 4, 6 or 8 boats
so there is much more chance of winning the end,
particularly when you consider half the fleet is trying to
help you. I'll look below at the strategic reasons for
doing it and how to go about it.

Starboard end – Why? – Diagram 3.4
Although winning the starboard end is difficult you
can achieve it by controlling both the speed of

approach and your height compared to the layline. If
you are attacked by a leeward boat you may have
difficulty. Why do it? Well the reason is **choice**. If one
of your boats **controls** the right-hand side of the start
line it is likely that for a period of time after the start
you will be in a position to prevent opposition boats
from tacking, thereby restricting their options. The
boat at the starboard end can see the whole fleet
clearly and can choose to tack off or hold on as suits
his team's position. Often the position may be held all
the way out to the port layline to the windward mark,
while team mates who have been able to tack off sail
fast up the beat.

The boat controlling the right of the pack has the
choice to tack on top of any opposition boats which
are ducking across behind him on port. The boat on
the right can also control whether boats are able to
make use of favourable windshifts or are forced to sail
on headers. Winning the starboard end of the line is
particularly useful when the beat is short since the cost
of ducking boats and missing shifts is very high, so all
the controlled boats are in a weak position. As the
distance sailed gets longer it becomes more likely that
a leeward boat will be able to get a leebow position or
even get far enough in front to tack and cross.

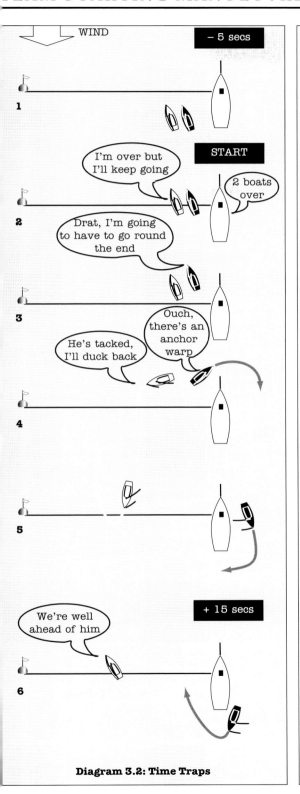

Diagram 3.2: Time Traps

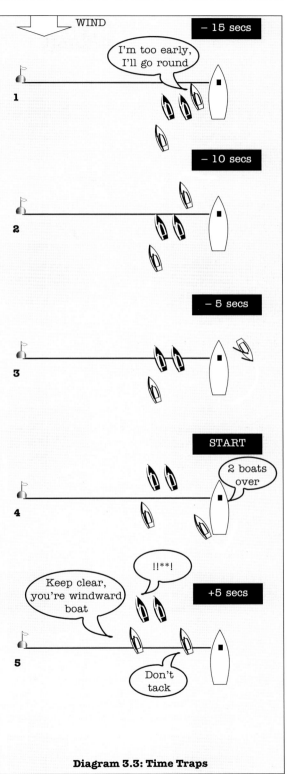

Diagram 3.3: Time Traps

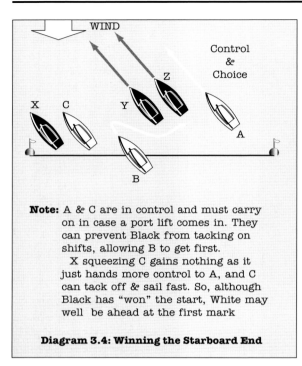

Note: A & C are in control and must carry on in case a port lift comes in. They can prevent Black from tacking on shifts, allowing B to get first.

X squeezing C gains nothing as it just hands more control to A, and C can tack off & sail fast. So, although Black has "won" the start, White may well be ahead at the first mark

Diagram 3.4: Winning the Starboard End

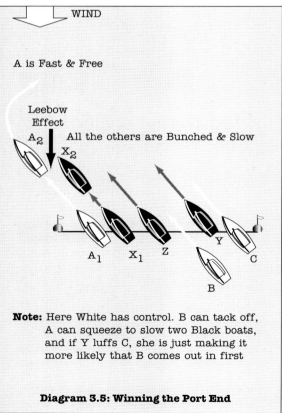

Note: Here White has control. B can tack off, A can squeeze to slow two Black boats, and if Y luffs C, she is just making it more likely that B comes out in first

Diagram 3.5: Winning the Port End

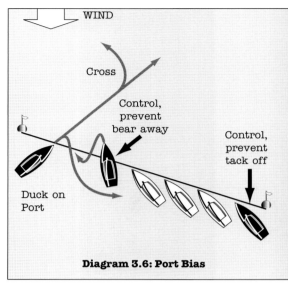

Diagram 3.6: Port Bias

Nevertheless, sailing slowly in a leebowed position may be best for your team as your team mates are going fast elsewhere.

Winning the port end – Why? – Diagram 3.5
The port end offers the potential to allow a boat to sail fast and free and therefore to accelerate easily. In boats where the leebow works well it is particularly important as you then squeeze up. The leebow is more difficult in wider boats like Vanguards. Start here if you can guarantee to go upwind well and can control the speed of approach accurately. The cost of being too early at the port end may well be to gybe around and cross behind the fleet on port tack. The risk of a weaker up-wind sailor starting here is that boats to windward will keep them trapped so they cannot tack. The potential benefits are that if a good start is made then the boat at the port end is often best placed to sail fastest since they can free-off to accelerate. This boat will then be in a good position to dominate the left hand side of the beat which might be favoured. They need to be able to break free of any boats above them before the layline is reached. They are exposed if the wind lifts on starboard since the boats above will get a safe windward position and will leave the port end starter a big loser.

3.1.3 Bad Starts – The great escapes
From time to time the approach, or the activities, of another boat will make your start go wrong. It might even be that you gave up a good start in favour of allowing one of your team mates to take pole position.

The first escape option to look at is driving on with good speed. It may be that you can get a good position

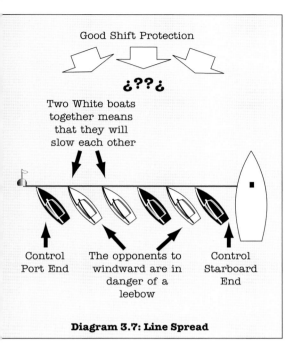

Diagram 3.7: Line Spread

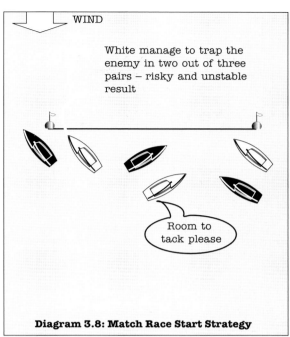

Diagram 3.8: Match Race Start Strategy

relative to other boats, and working with your team mates get through into the clear. Boats on top of you may themselves tack away, thus saving you the trouble.

If this is not looking hopeful because you are buried, then you can:

1. **Carry on sailing slowly in everyone's windshadow.**
2. **Drive off even further for speed and hope to gain clear air and a favourable windshift which will let you tack back onto port in a good position. The further you go to one side the more chance you may make a big gain (or loss).**
3. **Tack off to clear your air and open up more options.**

Option 1 is normally a bad move unless your position means you have got opposition boats trapped in even worse situations.

Option 2 can work well at the port end and on long beats where the boats will spread out.

Option 3, the tack off, is often used. When to tack out is a function of your skill in judging when you can do it without fouling another boat as you tack. If you are not the only member of your team to need to tack off to clear your air try to avoid the "own goal" of tacking simultaneously. It is better to agree who is going to escape first – the boat nearest the front of the fleet should have priority here. You should aim to be reasonably spaced apart from your team mates so it is harder for your opposition to control you.

3.2 ADVANCED STARTING

3.2.1 Team geographic start –
Diagrams 3.6 and 3.7

The basic options depicted show a way of spreading your boats around the line to get some advantage of line bias whilst keeping the boats spaced out so that you have some flexibility.

1. **Line spread** – Here your boats, spread out, beat all the opposition boats and are well positioned to respond to any shifts. If you approach the line and realise you are next to a team mate do something about it. With about 20 seconds to go there is still time to either:
   1. Gybe out and start further up the line in a gap, or,
   2. Bear away below an opponent or into a space away from your team mate.
2. **Port bias** – Here you partially commit the team to win the port end. Appreciate that in all likelihood it will not be possible for you all to do this so two of you actually concentrate on stopping the opposition. Note it is usually still worth having the most right hand boat to restrict the opposition's options. Be careful of a further left shift which may leave some of your team unable to lay the line on starboard tack.
3. **Starboard bias** – It will not be worth winning the port end at all. Two boats line up at different heights and with different line approach timing,

with the third coming in with a flexible approach, perhaps on port looking to tack into a gap. The two boats taking different approaches make winning the end more likely to be successful, but they must work well together to avoid closing either of them out or starting too early.

3.2.2 Match race starts – Diagram 3.8

As discussed in the pre-start section, boats often pair up with opposition boats in an effort to gain control. If your team decides to do this as a positive tactic it means you are going to sacrifice some control over the position of the boats on the start line. This risk is justified if you achieve control in at least two or three pairs and therefore have an advantage in those pairs as the line is approached. It will be difficult to tell who in each pair will win their start so it is still best to break off from a control situation with enough time to get back to the line and start well. This protects your team in the event that you lose some pairs and it also increases the chances of your winning combination being strong (e.g. 1st and 2nd).

The match race strategy is often used to take out a fast but inexperienced sailor in the other team. If they are not a strong tactical team racer but normally sail around in first place then they are a ripe target for a pre-start take out.

TOP TIPS – Starting

❍ Spread your boats out on the start line. Work hard to achieve good spacing during your approach

❍ Win key strategic points on the line such as the ends or the leeward position so you can leebow

❍ Look for ways to trap more than one opposition boat

❍ If you're controlling an opponent, only tack off if your team mates need help

❍ Be selfless with team mates in order to make sure your team gets at least two good starts

❍ Defend your leeward gap. Bear away to stop opponents going into it

❍ Keep close to the opposition on your windward side. You want to leebow them once on the beat

❍ Above all, accelerate off the line on time

UPWIND MANOEUVRES

.1 BASIC UPWIND MANOEUVRES

killful upwind boat-on-boat positioning will be the
eciding factor giving the ability to exert your
vindshadow to leeward, or through a leebow to
vindward, and the ability to control the manoeuvres of
ther boats by control zone positioning. Team racers will
ften need to deviate from the fastest course up the beat
o get into a position to slow or control an opponent.

Options on the beat are often a matter of making
ne best of the position you find yourself in. Boats in
articular patterns and positions lend themselves to
ertain manoeuvres. Realising your options early and
arrying out the necessary manoeuvre rapidly will gain
ne advantage for attacking or defending. A few
nches can make the difference between a successful
eebow on an opponent or being sailed over. You
eed to be able to sail the groove well (**see Skills**).

.1.1 The Squeeze – Diagram 4.1
his is a very satisfying manoeuvre to execute due to
ne teamwork involved. Team mates "sandwich" an
pponent. One uses blanketing skills to slow him while
lso controlling the situation by stopping the boat
om tacking off. The other boat to leeward gets into a
eebow position and slows the opposition boat further
nd stops her from bearing away to gain speed. It
vorks best if the leeward boat has luffing rights.

When done properly the squeeze can be used to
ring the leeward boat back into play from a position
vhere it was being controlled. The manoeuvre normally
oncludes with the squeezed boat dropping out of the
ack, then tacking, at which point the windward boat
acks straight on him so he cannot accelerate. This then
eleases the leeward boat to tack if it wishes; it will now
ave overtaken the squeezed boat.

The squeeze manoeuvre means that two boats from
ne team are engaged with one opposition boat. This
neans the key thing, especially on the first beat when
ne boats are close, is to do the manoeuvre quickly.

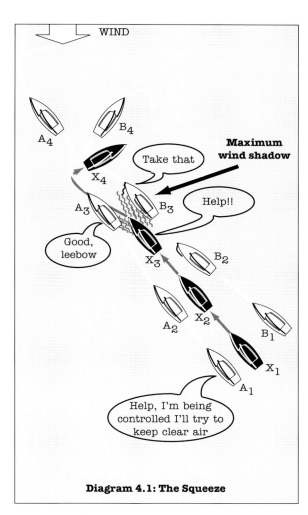

Diagram 4.1: The Squeeze

4.1.2 Covering
Covering refers to the method of staying ahead of an
opponent by tracking and copying all their moves. It
would normally mean that a boat stays between a
boat and the next mark. In team racing upwind
covering can be very aggressive and designed not just
to stay ahead of a boat but to slow its progress
upwind significantly.

4.1.2.1 The close cover
In this manoeuvre a boat locks on to an opponent and
focuses all its efforts on staying with them to slow them.
To get into this position a boat must get upwind of her
opponent and go onto the same tack. The "swoop down
and pin" is the method where a boat well to windward
drops down and quickly tries to trap the leeward boat
(Diagram 4.2). Surprise and good acceleration are critical
so the boat gets to the control zone as quickly as possible.

The close cover preventing a tack also starts to

GB Worlds Trials – Dave Derby (blue, right) and Jonny Mayhew (yellow, left) get into a tacking duel. Note the eased sails on Jonny's boat to enable her to accelerate quickly before going straight into the next tack

increase the problem for the covered boat. As they go past the layline the trap, known as a 'pin' or 'pick', is really costing Black time and places.

4.1.2.2 Tack out and prevention – Diagram 4.3
The most obvious way of avoiding being covered is to avoid being on the same tack. In order to tack out the leeward, attacked boat needs to do it early before the approaching opposition boat gets into the control zone. As soon as they are on opposite tacks and crossing one another the aggressor boat is restricted from hunting by Rule 16.2, **Changing Course** (which prevents the starboard boat forcing an immediate response from the port boat) so it is easier for the attacked boat to keep sailing fast.

To stop this tack out manoeuvre the initial aggressor should drop down quickly and not allow the tack to be put in. Once in a control position the distance between the boats needs to be maintained – small enough so the tack cannot be made but without getting so close that a luff or leebow by the leeward boat would be a risk. It is important that both boats are clear what luffing rights exist between them in this situation.

The leeward boat must know its luffing rights. If the leeward boat luffs up, as though it is attempting to tack, but then returns back to a close-hauled course the windward boat should protest unless the leeward

boat had got luffing rights under Rule 17.1, **On the Same Tack; Proper Course**. As leeward boat, if you do not have luffing rights any luff must be continued so you tack. If you did not have luffing rights but you luff and do not tack, you have broken Rule 17.1.

4.1.3 Tacking duel – Diagram 4.3
If the tack out is possible then it is inevitable that the leeward boat will want to try and obtain clean air by tacking. The leading opposition boat needs to then tack straight on top of the opponent if the position is to be maintained. This policy is most likely to invite the response of yet another tack from the covered boat, and on it goes.

If the lead boat can get down into a control zone then the tacking duel will stop. Otherwise both boats will be trying to get the best tacks. If the boat behind can do better roll tacks and get level it should try to go down the right hand side and then gain the initiative by tacking onto starboard, hopefully in a position where the other port boat, having slowed in the tacks, needs to tack immediately to avoid fouling by breaking Rule 10, **Opposite Tacks**.

Both boats will be doing over-rotating tacks. The windward boat does this to try and get down into the control zone, assuming it wants to trap the opponent.

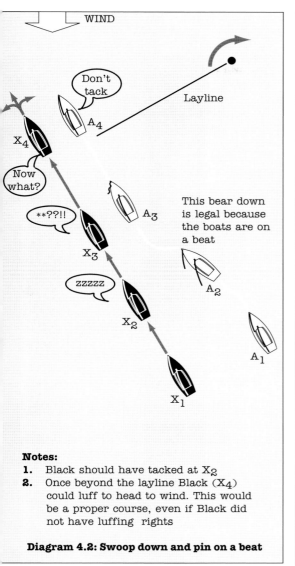

Notes:
1. Black should have tacked at X_2
2. Once beyond the layline Black (X_4) could luff to head to wind. This would be a proper course, even if Black did not have luffing rights

Diagram 4.2: Swoop down and pin on a beat

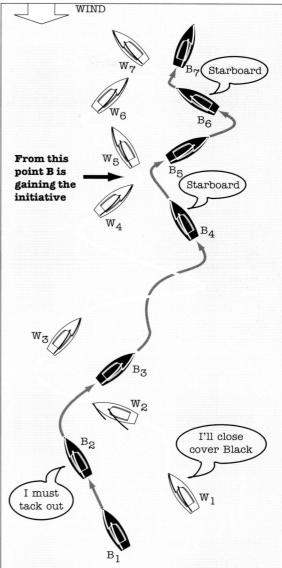

Through a series of tacks Black goes down the right-hand side, eventually catching White on port, forcing White to tack and gaining control of the situation and ultimately becoming the attacker rather than the defender

Diagram 4.3: The Tack Out & Tacking Duel

The leeward boat over-rotates to get clear enough to be able to turn and duck in the next tack and to accelerate. An 'over-rotating' tack is one where the boat turns beyond close hauled onto a reach. Be careful of how overlaps are acquired, especially if you are giving a leeward boat an overlap by your tack to windward of them. (Note: See Section 4.2.6, The Close Cover Tack and also Diagram 2.11 – Pre-Start Overlaps.)

4.1.4 Remote or loose cover – Diagram 4.4
Remote cover occurs when the covering boat is not in a control zone. These are the main reasons to do it:

1. To remain ahead of the opposition even in the event of a windshift.
2. To use windshadow skills to slow the opposing boat and therefore stretch or compress the race.
3. To monitor a situation and convert to a closer cover if some serious slowing of the

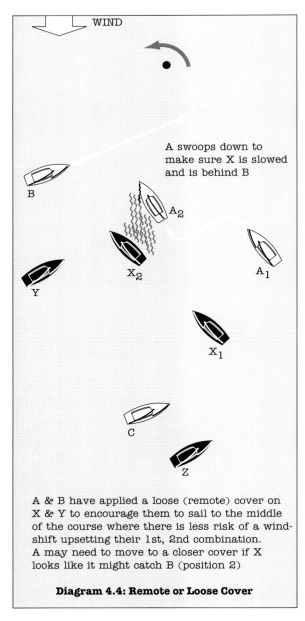

A swoops down to
make sure X is slowed
and is behind B

A & B have applied a loose (remote) cover on
X & Y to encourage them to sail to the middle
of the course where there is less risk of a windshift upsetting their 1st, 2nd combination.
A may need to move to a closer cover if X
looks like it might catch B (position 2)

Diagram 4.4: Remote or Loose Cover

**opposition is required with strong
windshadow.**

4.   **To encourage an opponent to go in a given
      direction.**

The remote cover can be achieved equally well by
placing the boat directly in front or even in a distant
leebow position. Depending on the location of the
next mark and the likely occurrence of any windshift
the leeward and ahead position can be an efficient
way of protecting your race position but it does not

allow you to swoop down and control your opponent
like a windward cover position.

Remote cover has the advantage that it is less likely
to result in a tacking duel, so the leading boat does
not risk being slowed or distracted by such antics.

In a remote cover situation both boats need to be
aware of how far away from the other boats the pair is
getting. As the pair go off to one side it becomes more
likely that some place changing will occur as they gain
leverage over the fleet.

The leading covering boat will try to avoid being
exposed by the pair going off to one side by "herding"
the covered opponent back to the middle of the course.
This is achieved by making the cover directly on the wind
of the trailing boat when they are going off to the side.
Conversely, when the covered boats tacks to head towards
the middle, the leading boat may choose to make the
tack not directly on her wind and this even "looser cover"
will hopefully mean they go in the desired direction.

The covered boat has a lot of options in a loose
cover situation. She can:
1.   Take a flier out to one side of the course in the hope
      that a big fleet gain is made through high leverage.
2.   Try to get the covering boat into a slowing tacking
      duel to distract it from the overall objective.
3.   Try to slow the lead boat by encouraging it to
      cover and then sailing on headers.
4.   Take the path of the covering boat towards other
      boats so it loses distance through management of
      crossing situations.
5.   Take the path of the covering boat towards your
      team members so that there are attacking options
      available to your team.

Thus in a loose cover situation the **trailing** boat has
far more initiative than in close covering.

4.1.5 Lee bow tack – Diagram 4.5

This situation is typically one where a port boat is
approaching a starboard boat and does not want to
duck. The lee-bow tack is better than a duck when:
1.   The boats are on or over the layline to the
      windward mark.
2.   The duck would be too expensive in terms of the
      ground given away, perhaps because other boats
      would also need to be ducked.
3.   The approaching port boat needs to slow the
      starboard boat.

After a leebow tack the boat to leeward has the
ability to control the speed of the two boats and can
use leebow and luffing to good effect. If it had chosen
to duck instead it could do neither of these things but
instead gets the advantage of being able to choose
when to tack which is best if the layline is uncertain.

The risks of carrying out the manoeuvre require a

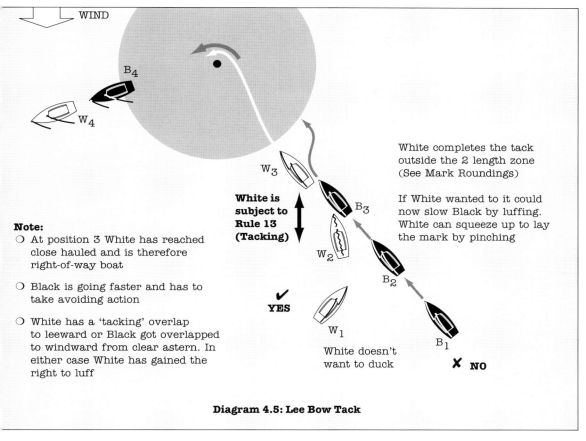

Diagram 4.5: Lee Bow Tack

The text within the diagram:

WIND

B₄

W₄

W₃

White completes the tack outside the 2 length zone (See Mark Roundings)

If White wanted to it could now slow Black by luffing. White can squeeze up to lay the mark by pinching

B₃

White is subject to Rule 13 (Tacking)

Note:

○ At position 3 White has reached close hauled and is therefore right-of-way boat

○ Black is going faster and has to take avoiding action

○ White has a 'tacking' overlap to leeward or Black got overlapped to windward from clear astern. In either case White has gained the right to luff

W₂

B₂

✔ YES

W₁

B₁

White doesn't want to duck

✘ NO

...ood appreciation of the transitions that the turning ...oat goes through. The transitions for White ...pproaching Black are as follows:

. White is port give-way boat.

. White is through head to wind and is give-way boat under Rule 13, **Changing Tacks**.

a. White completes the tack and is close hauled. Black then gets an overlap to windward of White from clear astern, **or**,

b. White completes its turn to close hauled while overlapped and gains instant rights with regard to Rule 11, **On The Same Tack, Overlapped**.

. White may luff but is subject to Rule 16.1, **Changing Course**.

. If they are not overlapped then Black is clear astern and subject to Rule 12, **On The Same Tack, Not Overlapped**.

...o in summary White remains burdened as give-way boat ...nder Rule 13, **Tacking** until it has got through to close ...auled. If they end up not overlapped it does not really ...ake much difference. Inevitably Black will now be going ...ster, it has now become the keep clear give-way boat ...ither as clear astern or as overlapped windward boat.

The rules do not define close hauled but it is taken to be when the boat is pointing on a normal 'close hauled' **course** angle – not necessarily having the sails filling or going at full speed. Transitions 3a and 3b are interchangeable since the overlap may well be gained after the turn is complete.

One possible option for the starboard boat is to bear away early to allow the port boat to cross. This is very difficult for the starboard boat to do without fouling under Rule 16.2, **Changing Course**. If it becomes obvious to a starboard boat that a leebow tack is happening then the best course of action is to luff hard once the port boat has committed to the tack. The effect of this is to increase the windward/leeward distance, minimising the leebow wind-shadow effect. It also makes it more difficult for any subsequent luff by the new leeward boat to be successful, since it will have to turn further and will therefore slow more.

A starboard boat may also want to leebow a port boat to avoid overstanding a mark or to protect the right hand side of the course. This is still a difficult manoeuvre since the starboard boat is, despite initially being right of way, additionally obliged not to impede

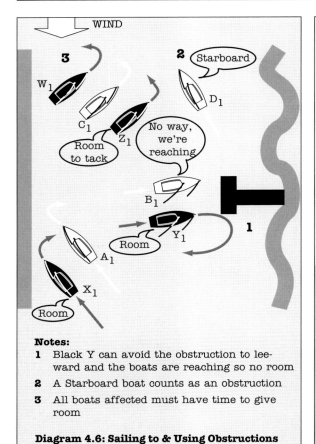

Notes:

1   Black Y can avoid the obstruction to leeward and the boats are reaching so no room

2   A Starboard boat counts as an obstruction

3   All boats affected must have time to give
room

Diagram 4.6: Sailing to & Using Obstructions

The Committee boat IS an obstruction – SO
ROOM **IS** ALLOWED

The Committee boat IS NOT an obstruction if
approaching the line to start – SO ROOM **IS
NOT** ALLOWED

Diagram 4.7: Sailing to & Using Obstructions

the port boat as the starboard boat turns to head to wind
(Rule 16.2, **Changing Course**) and after going through
head-to-wind it is give-way tacking boat (Rule 13) just
as in the scenario above. In addition the port boat can
alter course to reduce the starboard boat's room to tack.
The port boat can do this because it is not restricted by
Rule 16.2, **Changing Course**. The port boat cannot
force a collision with the approaching tacking boat or it
may have broken Rule 16.1, **Changing Course** as it is
right of way (on port tack) over give way (tacking) so
must, when changing course, provide room.

Tip:

1.   Don't risk tacking too close when doing a lee
bow tack

2.   Don't lee bow tack if you are going to need
to tack again and you only have a short
distance to the layline

4.1.6 Using obstructions – Diagrams 4.6 & 4.7
This section concerns the use of Rule 19, **Room to
Tack at an Obstruction**, as a way of breaking a difficult

cover or stopping another boat controlling you.
   As a close-covered leeward boat the proximity of an
obstruction (a shore or right-of-way boat) is an
opportunity to force the windward boat to tack. You
must make sure that you fulfil the requirements of the
Rule, namely that:

1.   The boats are **close hauled**.

2.   It really is an obstruction requiring a **substantial**
alteration of course.

3.   You really could not tack to keep clear of the
obstruction (and also manage to keep clear of the
other boat by ducking) **unless** it gives you room.

4.   You must ask in time for it to be **possible** for you
to be given room, allowing for a reasonable

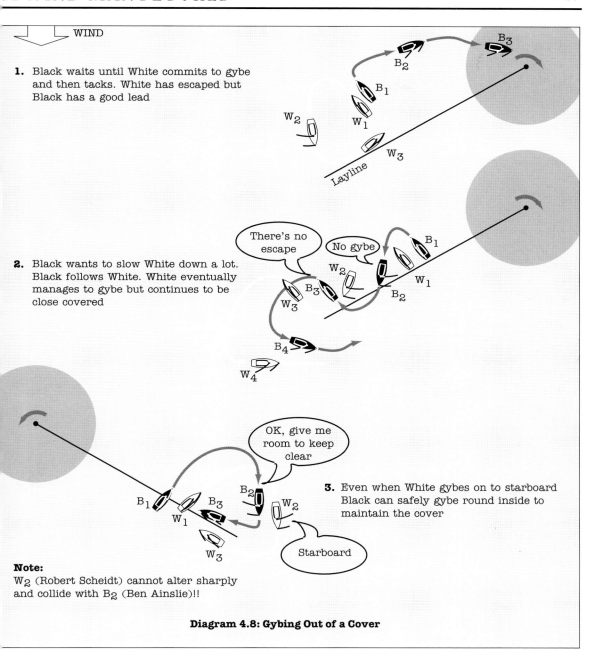

WIND

1. Black waits until White commits to gybe and then tacks. White has escaped but Black has a good lead

2. Black wants to slow White down a lot. Black follows White. White eventually manages to gybe but continues to be close covered

There's no escape

No gybe

OK, give me room to keep clear

3. Even when White gybes on to starboard Black can safely gybe round inside to maintain the cover

Starboard

Note:
W₂ (Robert Scheidt) cannot alter sharply and collide with B₂ (Ben Ainslie)!!

Diagram 4.8: Gybing Out of a Cover

response time and not expecting any extraordinary or abnormal sailing from the other boat.

You must tack as soon as possible after the other boat tacks.

Note that if the boat to windward, which has been hailed for "room to tack", replies to the request for room by hailing "You Tack" (Rule 19.1(b)) then the windward boat has exposed itself to a potential incident. If the leeward boat now hits the windward boat at any stage then the windward boat will be deemed not to have given sufficient room. The windward boat should therefore avoid replying "You Tack" unless it is certain it will be in a situation where it will remain clear. As soon as you reply "You Tack" you give yourself an extra burden (interpretation of Rule 19.1(b)).

Sometimes boats get caught up before the start and end up sailing towards a committee boat or mark. They can call for room to pass or tack for the obstruction if

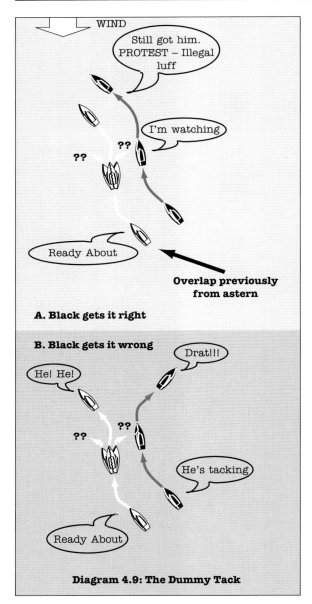

Diagram 4.9: The Dummy Tack

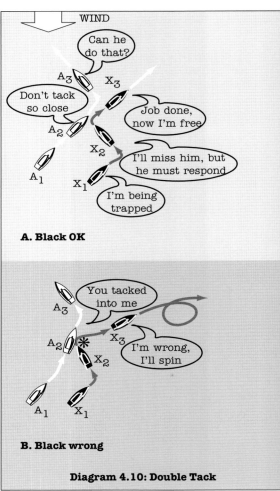

Diagram 4.10: Double Tack

Rule 18, Passing Obstructions or Rule 19, Room to Tack at an Obstruction, applies. They would have to be going upwind on a close hauled course for Rule 19 to apply.

While committee boats are big and hard they are specifically excluded from counting as obstructions if they are a starting mark, surrounded by navigable water and the boats are **approaching the line to start**. Do not call for 'room' on committee boats when starting; if you do then expect to be protested, you are 'barging'.

Remember that even if you are in the right and another boat calls for room incorrectly you still have to

respond. If you respond and then protest this is safer than forcing a collision. The umpires (and your opponent) would take a dim view of shutting a boat out and forcing a collision with a large obstruction.

4.2 ADVANCED UPWIND MANOEUVRES

4.2.1 Gybe out of a close cover

Assume a boat is being covered closely and decides that it must escape. The leeward boat can gybe round onto the other tack, enabling it to head towards the mark. This manoeuvre may also mean that the close cover is broken. If the covering boat does not attempt to follow it might be quicker, once it is obvious the covering boat isn't bearing away, to change the plan and tack instead. This is because the gybe around, particularly in strong wind, can be a costly manoeuvre in terms of distance lost. In boats like Fireflies in medium winds the gybe can be

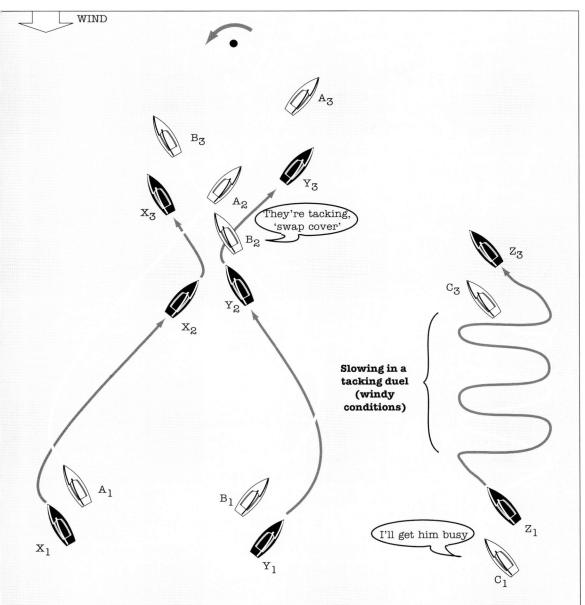

- White C distracts Black Z (who is in contention for 1st) and gets Z involved in a tacking duel
- Meanwhile White A & B sail fast
- Overall White gain. White A & B cross each other rather than tacking. By swapping cover partners they increase distance
- A_3 should slow Y_3 to make sure B_3 can get to the mark ahead

Diagram 4.11: Managing The Pairs – Slowing Tactics from Behind

completed very effectively losing a minimum of distance.
  The risk associated with gybing out of a cover is that
the covering boat will follow. It will try to turn more
sharply and prevent the gybe and force the covered
boat to continue sailing away from the windward mark.
An alternative scenario, particularly if gybing onto

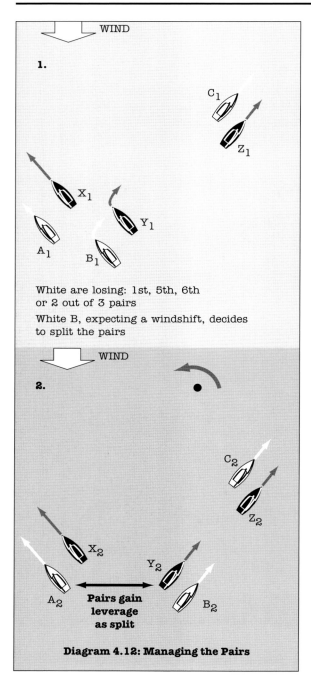

White are losing: 1st, 5th, 6th
or 2 out of 3 pairs

White B, expecting a windshift, decides
to split the pairs

Diagram 4.12: Managing the Pairs

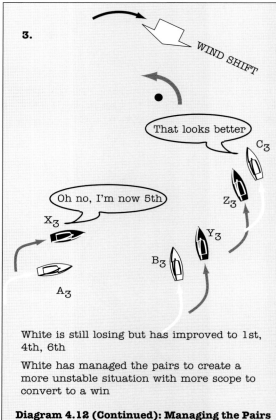

White is still losing but has improved to 1st,
4th, 6th

White has managed the pairs to create a
more unstable situation with more scope to
convert to a win

Diagram 4.12 (Continued): Managing the Pairs

4.8 (3)). As this is such a big manoeuvre it is worth the
leeward boat trying some large bear aways followed by
luffs to try and break the close cover through good boat
control before committing to the gybe.

If you are trying to gybe out, so that you can get to
the finish, wait to do the manoeuvre until you are
certain you will be able to lay the finish line.

4.2.2 Dummy tack – Diagram 4.9
If the cover is quite close but a tack is possible then it
can work well to feign a tack and revert back onto the
original course. If the trailing boat watches the lead
boat then it can choose to make it a dummy tack at a
late stage. It might be that the covering boat will spot
the tactic and stop mid-tack. A period of hovering at
head to wind may then occur. The crew and helm
who can work together best will do well here. Once a
commitment is made, either to return to the original
tack or to continue to the new tack, the crew needs to
back the jib to help the turn since the boats will now
be moving much slower (see Diagram 4.9).

It is an important rule point that if a leeward boat luffs

starboard, is that the covering boat turns inside and is
then confronted with a boat that has gybed onto
starboard and is now coming back up to close hauled as
a right-of-way boat. The port tack give-way boat may
then continue the turn and gybe as well but only if this
response is consistent with its best efforts to keep clear as
opposed to luffing behind the starboard boat (Diagram

nd does not then become 'clear astern', this could
reak Rule 17.1, **On the Same Tack: Proper Course,**
vhich states that a leeward boat which obtained an
overlap from clear astern shall not sail above her proper
ourse during that overlap unless in doing so she
promptly sails astern of the other boat. So if a boat goes
or the tack but cannot make it then it may have broken
Rule 17.1. This means that it is critical that both boats
and the umpires) know whether the boats are in an
overlap which has given the leeward boat luffing rights.

4.2.3 Double tack – Diagram 4.10

This technique is quite an extreme manoeuvre. A covered
port tack boat tacks onto starboard but is so close to the
covering boat that a collision becomes a high risk. If the
situation then resulted in a collision the tacking boat has
broken her obligations under Rule 15, **Acquiring Right
of Way** (Diagram 4.10). If it had not even got through to
being on close hauled then Rule 13, **Tacking** is relevant
since the boat has not completed passing between head
to wind and close hauled so is not entitled to any rights
over the port tack boat.

In this scenario (Diagram 4.10.A) it is assumed
that the tacking boat has completed a clean tack, so
the port tack boat now has to start responding
immediately, trying to keep clear of the new right-of-
way boat. The initiating, leeward boat has not given
sufficient room and knowing that it would therefore
break Rule 15 it now responds by tacking back onto
port underneath the now luffing and tacking opposition
boat. The desired result will be that the original covering
boat has tacked off. Alternatively the boats will simply
be closer together and on the same tack.

If the incident is seen by umpires to result in a collision
then the initiating leeward boat will probably receive a
penalty. If the manoeuvre is completed without a
collision then it is most likely they will take the view that
no rule has been broken since both boats have met their
respective rule obligations.

4.2.4 Managing the Pairs – Team Covering

Once boats are covering each other it becomes a boat-
on-boat duel. It is easy to make the mistake of losing the
overview of the race. You should be asking yourselves:

◯ Is it important that I keep my position in the race?
◯ I am leading the pair, do I want to perform
   manoeuvres that make us:
   ❏ go slowly?
   ❏ go quickly?
   ❏ go a particular way?
◯ I am losing the pair, if I remain covered do I:
   ❏ go slowly?
   ❏ go quickly?
   ❏ go a particular way?

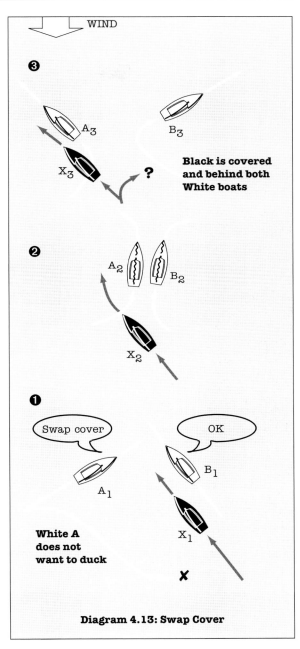

**Black is covered
and behind both
White boats**

Swap cover

OK

**White A
does not
want to duck**

Diagram 4.13: Swap Cover

In answering these questions both boats will be
aware of the importance of their position for the team
combination. Can the team make better ground by trying
to get out of covering or should the pairs look at the
options whilst staying paired up. This involves seeing how
the race changes when pairs of boats overtake other
pairs of boats. This can easily convert a stable combination
into an unstable one. The best way of managing this
situation so that pairs **do overtake** each other is to:

GB Worlds Trials – They cover each other… "If you tack I will tack" the lead boat is thinking

○ Deliberately sail some pairs fast by sailing lifts, going the right way and not tacking too much.
○ Deliberately sail the other pair slowly by tacking a lot, going the wrong way and sailing headers (Diagram 4.11).
○ Pushing the pairs to opposite sides of the course in shifty conditions and therefore gaining high leverage across the fleet (Diagram 4.12 – 1, 2 & 3).

Note that if the weather is light and the roll tacks are good it can be that boats engaged in legitimate tacking duels are easily able to keep up with boats which are not tacking.

By contrast the way to keep pairs **close** and therefore keep the advantage with the leading team is to:
○ Keep the pairs always sailing at the same speed. If a pair is going too fast tack more and tighten the cover, if a pair is going too slowly then loosen the cover and sail more on the lifts.
○ Keep the pairs sailing in the middle of the course so that the race is in balance. If the boats are heading away from the middle then apply a strong windshadow (or if behind, tack) and if they are going towards the middle keep the cover loose so that leeward boats do not have to clear their air immediately. Thus you try to 'herd' the game toward the middle of the course.

Tips:
1. If leading 2 pairs keep near the middle of the beat
2. If losing 2 pairs, separate the pairs and try to go fast/slow to promote overtaking

4.2.5 Swap Cover and Cannot Tack –
Diagram 4.13

In this manoeuvre two boats of the same team are approaching on opposite tacks. One or both of the boats are engaged in a cover on an opponent. In order to avoid ducking one another, which gives distance away and also may not be possible, the two boats swap cover by both tacking close to each other in such a way that they take over each other's course. In the example shown this saves White A from having to duck the black boat and so avoids a place being lost.

To perform the manoeuvre successfully both boats must be aware of the situation and the final call as to what is to happen should lie with the boat which otherwise is going to duck since she is the most exposed if the manoeuvre goes wrong or is not required. This is a manoeuvre where two boats work together to leave their opponent little scope for action. If the covered boat tacks off it will simply continue to

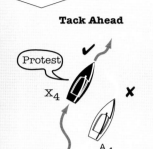

Tack Ahead

4. White luffs, Black protests

3. Black completes tack clear ahead

2. Black tacks

Note big gap

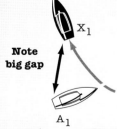

1. White ducks Black

Black tacks into an overlap & can be luffed

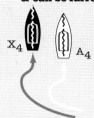

4. White can luff Black

3. White gains an overlap during the tack

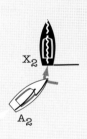

2. As Black goes through head to wind, White is clear astern

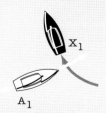

1. White ducks Black

Forced to tack back

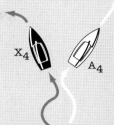

4. White's persistent & heavy luff forces Black to tack back

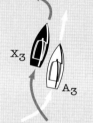

White holds her course

3. The instantaneous overlap means White has the right to luff. In addition, Black is still tacking. Black may have to go back onto starboard

2. When Black goes through head to wind White is already overlapped

1. White luffs hard as it crosses Black's transom

Diagram 4.14: The Close Tack – Formerly Known as The Slam Dunk

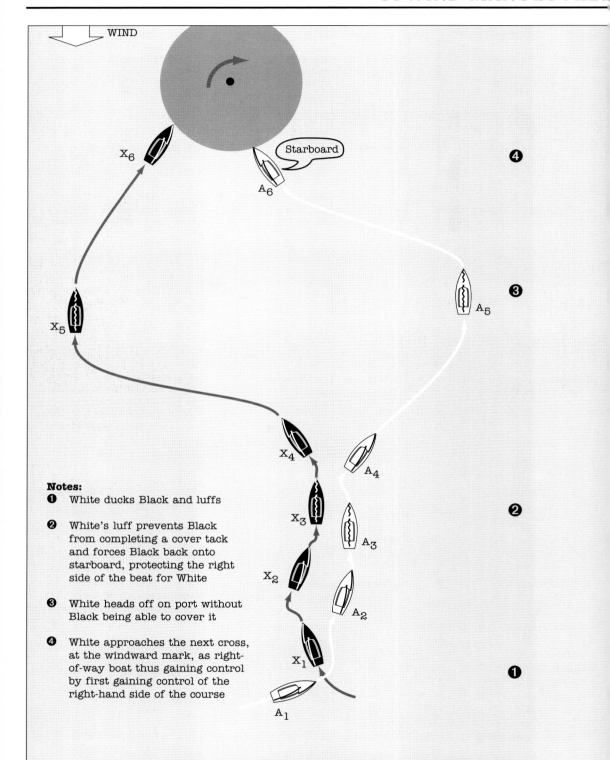

Notes:

❶ White ducks Black and luffs

❷ White's luff prevents Black from completing a cover tack and forces Black back onto starboard, protecting the right side of the beat for White

❸ White heads off on port without Black being able to cover it

❹ White approaches the next cross, at the windward mark, as right-of-way boat thus gaining control by first gaining control of the right-hand side of the course

Diagram 4.15: Tactical Use of the 'Close Duck' to 'Control the Right'

Worlds – The storm comes through but racing goes on with the help of reduced cut sails. This team have a big lead and will cover both sides of the beat keeping all three boats near the front of the race in case of gear failure or capsize

be covered by the same boat.

The swap cover works equally well if both boats were covering opponents. You avoid wasteful ducking whilst the opposition remain covered.

4.2.6 The Close Cover Tack/The Close Duck – Slam Dunk of Old

This manoeuvre takes place when boats are crossing on a beat and one boat decides to try and tack on top of the other (Diagram 4.14).

The objectives for the tacking boat (Black) are:

1. To gain **control** of the other boat by getting on to the same tack as it and therefore being in phase with any shifts that boat gets and so making staying in front more certain.
2. To use the control gained to potentially **slow** the now leeward boat by windshadow and by trying to prevent the other boat from tacking.
3. To avoid any incident where, as the **tacking boat** (constrained by Rule 13, Tacking), it is **required to keep clear** of the ducking boat who may luff up head-to-wind.

4. To avoid being threatened as the new **windward boat** (burdened by Rule 11, On the Same Tack Overlapped). This is made difficult because it is likely the windward boat is now **exposed to a luff** by the leeward boat under rights gained under a clause in Rule 17.1, On the Same Tack; Proper Course – see particularly the last sentence of this rule which states "this rule (Rule 17.1) does NOT apply if the overlap begins while the windward boat is required by Rule 13 to keep clear". (An overlap gained by a boat tacking on top of another boat.)

Note: The clause from Rule 17.1 cited above **is new to the 2001 Rules** and as such makes the traditional slam dunk manoeuvre very hazardous for the tacking boat. For much of the manoeuvre and immediately after it, the tacking boat is vulnerable.

The objectives for the ducking boat (White) are:

1. To try and avoid a control position being gained by the tacking boat. Therefore, it is good to avoid getting on the same tack as the other boat. In simple terms, a smart move is to watch the boat crossing you committing to its tack and then

simply **tacking off immediately**. This will ensure that you are not covered so the only slowing will occur if you now slow due to tacking or receive a bad windshift. The covering boat will struggle to tack back straight away as it may be slowed from its first tack. This sequence of events is likely to result in a tacking duel.

2. The ducking boat wants to stop the crossing boat tacking so close to it that it will be able to pin or prevent a tack out. To do this the ducking boat, if close enough, can luff up above close-hauled as the crossing boat clears it. As the crossing boat goes through head-to-wind it becomes a tacking boat (Rule 13, **Tacking**) and the ducking boat is now right of way and is able to try and **prevent the tacking boat from completing its tack** as long as it does not foul under Rule 16, **Changing Course**. The tacking boat may well have to reverse its turn and go back onto the original tack.

3. If the leading, crossing boat does manage to complete its tack by getting to close-hauled it is important to both boats to **know if an overlap exists**. If it exists at this time it was gained from clear astern whilst the crossing boat completed its tack. This means the leeward boat has the right to luff (subject to Rule 16, **Changing Course**). **It should luff** to try and force the windward boat to tack away, to slow them down, or to give it a penalty under Rule 11, **On the Same Tack, Overlapped**.

4. If the crossing boat completes its tack and is so far ahead that it manages to get to close-hauled **clear ahead** then in reality the boats are quite well spaced. In this situation, unless it wants to be trapped, the leeward boat should **tack out**. Really it should have tacked sooner because it will now be possible for the covering boat to stay with it and keep in phase when the trailing boat tacks.

Conclusion
Due to the risks of tacking and due to the likelihood of being exposed to a luff, it is difficult for the crossing boat to achieve a close tack. The tacking boat should therefore **give some space** by delaying the cover tack adequately after crossing. If the covering boat now bears away sharply and the covered boat delays its response then the covering boat may still be able to get into the control zone without risk.

As the ducking boat you are quite well placed and indeed should **use a close duck as a powerful weapon**, particularly when a port boat ducks a starboard boat. Having ducked you can prevent a close cover tack and then gain **control of the right hand side** of the course and thereby hope to approach the windward objective with right-of-way after having tacked onto starboard (Diagram 4.15).

It is, therefore, important to see this set of manoeuvres in the context of what happens overall on a beat and how the exchange of control in a pair of crossing boats can so often reverse control and positions at a critical point in a race. Practise it…

Diagram 4.14 shows some of the scenarios that occur most frequently.

5

REACHING MANOEUVRES

.1 REACHING MANOEUVRES

he reaching legs need to be viewed in the context of
he whole race. If the reach immediately precedes a run
ind you are in a close but leading position it may be in
our team's interests that the boats are well spaced out
is they go onto the run in order to make opponents'
windshadows from behind less effective. This would be
particularly true of the first boat in a 1:4:5 combination.
Because the run is so important this may be an overriding
actor and dictate your reaching tactics, forcing a more
conservative approach.

If the reach is just before the last beat and the race is
till in an unstable combination then both teams will
be attacking. This will mean the boats bunch up. The
eaching tactics are therefore more aggressive on some
eaching legs than others.

5.1.1 Room?

he simplest way of overtaking a boat on a reach is to
ail down the leg and at the end of it make sure you have
gained an overlap on the inside for the mark. You can
hen use Rule 18, **Passing Marks and Obstructions**, to
obtain room to round the mark ahead of the other
boat. Naturally if you get an overlap to windward you
are likely to be luffed before you get to the two length
zone. This manoeuvre therefore works best when the
next mark is to be rounded to leeward. This is most
elevant on a broad reach/run where boats ahead are
slowed by windshadow and are therefore most likely
o have overlaps gained on them from astern.

5.1.2 Reaching: Leading Boat Attacks to
Windward
Summary:
Preparation: 1. Slow/bear away
            2. Trap boat astern to windward of you

Attack: 3. Luff
            4. Control

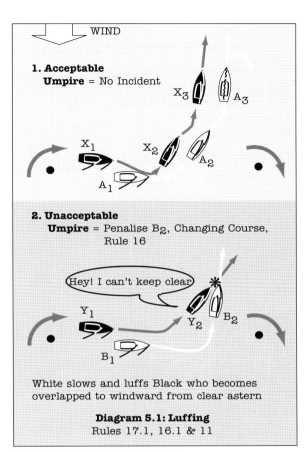

1. Acceptable
  Umpire = No Incident

2. Unacceptable
  Umpire = Penalise B₂, Changing Course,
           Rule 16

Hey! I can't keep clear

White slows and luffs Black who becomes
overlapped to windward from clear astern

Diagram 5.1: Luffing
Rules 17.1, 16.1 & 11

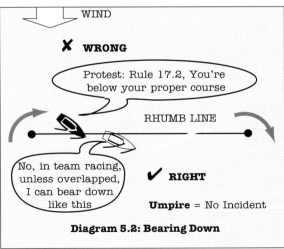

✗ **WRONG**

Protest: Rule 17.2, You're
below your proper course

RHUMB LINE

No, in team racing,
unless overlapped,
I can bear down
like this

✔ **RIGHT**

Umpire = No Incident

Diagram 5.2: Bearing Down

As leading boat on a reach you often want to trap a
boat behind to let your team mates catch up. If you
have to bear away round the next mark it will be particularly helpful to trap your opponent to windward so
that it is then easier for your team mates to get an inside

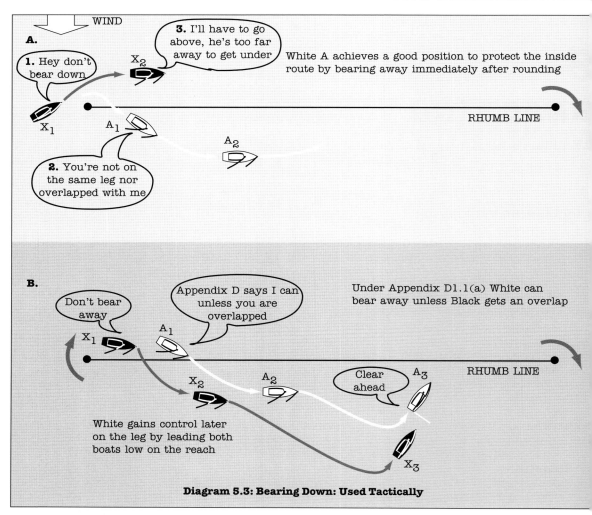

Diagram 5.3: Bearing Down: Used Tactically

overlap. Even if you are heading up at the next mark, trapping a boat in a luff is a useful offensive manoeuvre as you can control both your own progress and that of your opponent quite easily as leeward right-of-way boat.

Slowing, trapping a boat to windward then luffing is a simple manoeuvre sequence where the new leeward boat can turn to windward when overlapped as long as it remains aware of the management of the incident such that the other boat's response and the application of Rule 16, **Changing Course** are kept in balance. It is not realistic to expect to give a windward boat a penalty unless they are very slow in responding or get too close to the leeward boat when coming in from astern. The luff manoeuvre should be used to control the opponent, not hit them.

In order to prepare for the luff it is desirable to be below the rhumb line to the next mark so that the boat approaching from behind will find it more difficult

to go to leeward.

Note that in Appendix D1.1(a) team racing has a slightly different version of Rule 17.2. In this version the boat bearing down below its proper course only breaks Rule 17.2 if the other boat is actually **overlapped to leeward** (as opposed to steering a course to leeward within two lengths).

Having forced a boat to go to windward you are now in a position to use Rule 11, **On the Same Tack Overlapped** as an attacking weapon. It is important to judge how high to luff since this will influence the overall success. If there is a danger that the boat overlapped to windward may break through and get clear ahead then the leeward boat should luff higher and if necessary up to head to wind. If the objective is just to keep the boat trapped to windward then a close reach will do since this gives optimum control of speed and therefore makes it difficult for the windward boat to

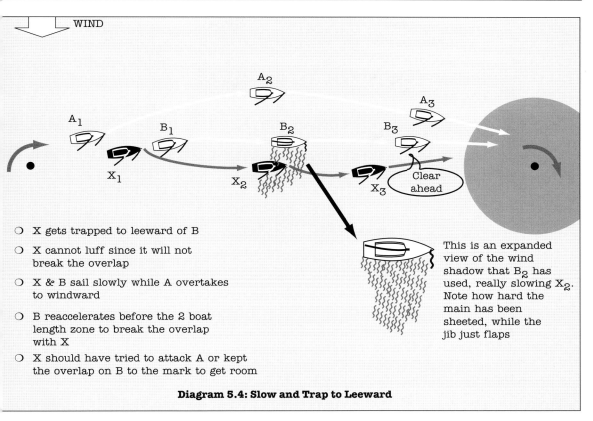

WIND

A₂

A₃

A₁

B₁

B₂

B₃

X₁

X₂

X₃

Clear ahead

○ X gets trapped to leeward of B

○ X cannot luff since it will not break the overlap

○ X & B sail slowly while A overtakes to windward

○ B reaccelerates before the 2 boat length zone to break the overlap with X

○ X should have tried to attack A or kept the overlap on B to the mark to get room

This is an expanded view of the wind shadow that B₂ has used, really slowing X₂. Note how hard the main has been sheeted, while the jib just flaps

Diagram 5.4: Slow and Trap to Leeward

slip out of the luff which she might try to do by slowing sharply and trying to go to leeward.

The luff to windward can work well on all types of reach and in all conditions. You should always be careful not to slow too much in planing conditions since a boat might be able to break through over the top very quickly indeed. Sail high and early if you are approaching a boat from behind and intend to go to windward. At least then the leeward boat will have to make a special effort to come and get you.

5.1.3 Slow and trap to leeward – Diagram 5.4

Often the boat approaching from behind will avoid getting overlapped to windward despite aggressive bearing away by the lead clear-ahead boat. The boats may well sail very low as the lead boat tries to slow progress down the reach. The leg may even become a beat at the end as the boats go beyond the layline having sailed so far to leeward (see Diagram 5.3B).

If the lead boat does allow or force a boat to leeward of it, and then sails a course to keep the boats overlapped, then both boats will proceed along the proper course. The snag for the boat to leeward is that the windward boat will use windshadow techniques to make both of them go very slowly (Diagram 5.4). As

the boat is now trapped to leeward, team mates of the lead boat may sail over the top with conviction in the knowledge they cannot be luffed. Only if the leeward boat can break the overlap and luff to a clear astern position (Rule 17.1) can it expect to regain the freedom needed to luff boats approaching from behind.

So, the leading boat on a reach has a leeward slowing option. As long as it remains clear ahead it can drag a boat behind down to leeward, since the boat behind will be living in fear of a luff if it dares to go to windward. As the boat behind, under threat of being stopped, this is a moment when it is much better to work with a team mate. If you are on your own then your best bet will be to attack the enemy astern of you and avoid confrontation with the enemy in front.

> **Tip:**
> ○ Enemy in front and enemy behind you –
> **Attack the one behind you**

5.1.4 Working together – the "High–Low" – Diagrams 5.5 & 5.6

This manoeuvre is one where two trailing boats round the windward mark behind an opponent and the first one goes to windward (high) and the second to

Worlds – Power Reach. USA in blue have N° 14 going to sail high to protect her position from the threat of N°18 His team mates in N°15 drive off hoping to get clear ahead

Wilson 2000 – On the top reach. GBR in yellow (N° 19 & 21) have 1st (out of the photo), 2nd & 3rd. With the run still to come the USA team in blue (N° 22, 23 & 24) need to be stopped. So N°21 (your author!) bears away to get to leeward so that the USA sailors will be forced to go high and can then be luffed. Note the wake from the umpire boats which can be used for promoting surfing if the sailors concentrate on it

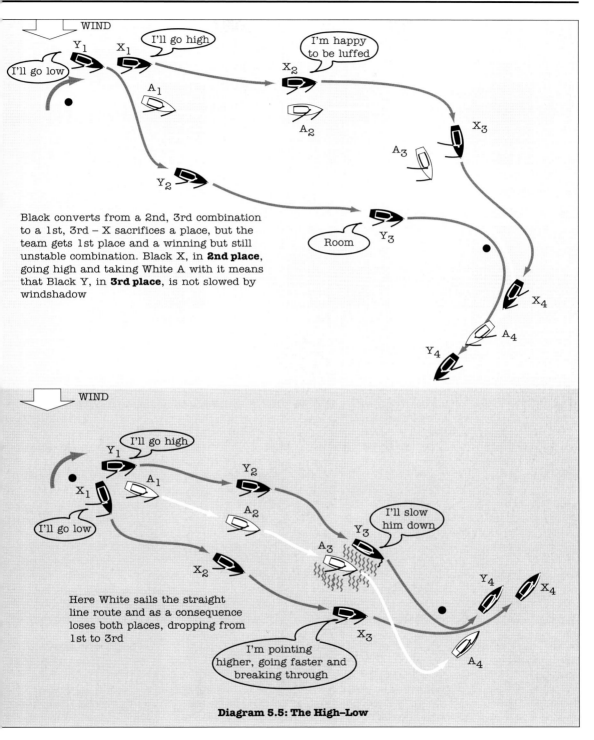

Black converts from a 2nd, 3rd combination to a 1st, 3rd – X sacrifices a place, but the team gets 1st place and a winning but still unstable combination. Black X, in **2nd place**, going high and taking White A with it means that Black Y, in **3rd place**, is not slowed by windshadow

Here White sails the straight line route and as a consequence loses both places, dropping from 1st to 3rd

Diagram 5.5: The High–Low

eward (low). (The other options would be both oing high, both going low or the first boat going low nd the second high.) Disadvantages are:

1. BOTH HIGH – potentially you both get luffed by the opponent;
2. BOTH LOW – potentially both get windshadow; and

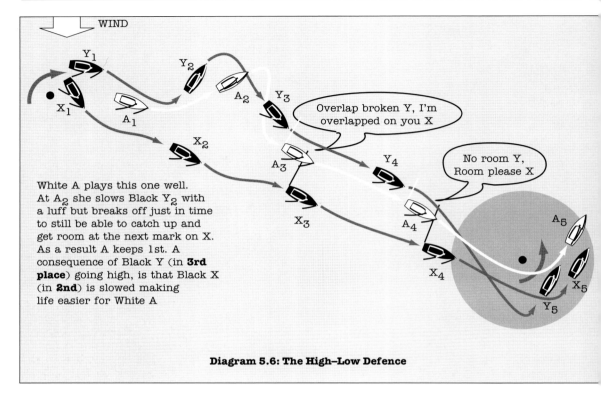

White A plays this one well. At A$_2$ she slows Black Y$_2$ with a luff but breaks off just in time to still be able to catch up and get room at the next mark on X. As a result A keeps 1st. A consequence of Black Y (in **3rd place**) going high, is that Black X (in **2nd**) is slowed making life easier for White A

Overlap broken Y, I'm overlapped on you X

No room Y, Room please X

Diagram 5.6: The High–Low Defence

3. Low/HIGH – this delays the desired slowing effect of getting the enemy in front to luff one of you.

The first boat to get close to the opponent sails immediately to a windward overlap and entices the boat to luff it. The second boat goes to leeward and drives through on or just below the rhumb line, with clearer wind as the opposition boat goes off to windward. If the lead boat tries to play both boats he will find they separate and as they are both largely unaffected one of them will find it easier to get an overlap by the end of the leg.

What should the lead boat do to defend? She initially does best by attacking the boat which is going down the inside route to the next mark to block the chance of their getting room at the mark, and then breaks off to try and prevent the other boat getting right through. If the high/low pair make the mistake of keeping too close together then the lead boat will be able to encourage them to affect each other with windshadow.

If the lead boat can it should take the reach low so that there is more control towards the end of the leg when it really matters who has and has not got an overlap. The converse of this point is that the high/low works particularly well on a broad reach when blanketing from the overtaking windward boat is especially effective.

5.1.5 Breaking the overlap – Diagram 5.7
Once a boat has been trapped to windward with the leeward boat having full luffing rights then the main concern for the windward boat is the ability of the boat to leeward to luff so far. The windward attacked boat needs to break the overlap if possible and recreate it with the leeward boat having come in from clear astern. If the boats are suitably positioned this can be achieved by the windward boat turning to windward so that the line of its transom is clear ahead. Actually a line parallel to the transom across the aftmost point, probably the rudder. If one boat is clear astern then by definition the other boat is clear ahead. This can be confusing since the boat to windward is still level with parts of the other boat. Remember that it is the transom line and clear astern that count (see definitions).

Once the overlap is recreated by the resumption of a proper course by the windward boat the new overlap is "from clear astern" since the last position of the leeward boat was indeed clear astern. This means that the leeward boat has no luffing rights.

When the leeward boat sees you are committed to a big luff to break the overlap it gains handsomely in terms of distance by bearing away. It then, additionally, has the option of gybing twice and reacquiring luffing rights on you. The reach would have to be broad for this to work – see Running.

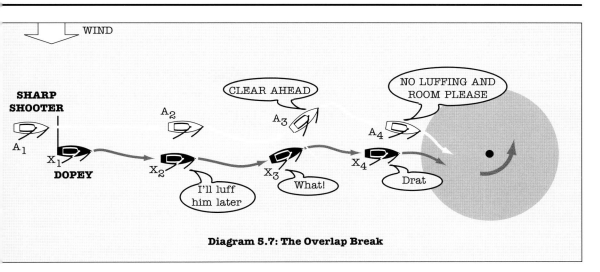

Diagram 5.7: The Overlap Break

5.1.6 The Stages of the Reach

You should be careful to look at which are the important boats for your team **before** you get on to the reach. Which boats are at the Focus? Who do you need to overtake? Can you afford to be luffed by the opponent ahead of you? Remember that two boats from one team can work well together when going downwind since the opposition boat ahead will find it a challenge to slow both of them at once. When on the reach you need to decide, are you slowing the race down or trying to go forward? If you are losing and unstable you may well want to slow the reach and try and convert. If you are stable and ahead, or simply ahead and well placed, you may well not want to risk stopping or slowing.

5.1.6.1 Tactical considerations

Set up – As you leave the windward mark or turn on to a reach from a run you need to be positioning your boat for the future leg. Things to consider are:

- Getting into a position to luff. You may be able bear away to then trap an opponent to windward.
- Keeping clear of your team by agreeing who is going high or low to avoid each other's windshadows. Always look at the most **threatened** boat on your team and make sure they can sail the safest course and build in the other boats' course options after that.
- Implement the high/low manoeuvre at this stage if the situation is suitable.

Mid reach – During the middle of the leg an experienced sailor will already be able to read the pattern of the boats and have a very good idea of who is likely to get which positions by the two length circle. If that result is not going to be good enough

some further aggressive action will be required. If you are happy with your position then just go fast.

Going fast means being aware of the rhumb line and only deviating from it if there is a tactical advantage.

Key tactical manoeuvres to do at this stage are pass-backs by using windshadow or luffs. If you are the aggressor, force your opponent to get an overlap on you. Once overlapped you can force him to sit in your windshadow, or luff him depending on which side he is trapped.

End of reach – After all the action down the reach the really exciting bit comes as the boats grapple to see who will have room at the next mark. You have to be realistic here and bear in mind the onus on a boat changing an overlap to **prove it**. It is worth being outspoken and making sure your competitors and the umpires know for sure about the status is of any overlaps you are involved in. Things to be aware of…

- It can be hard to retain overlaps at, or just before, the two length zone. Make sure you are certain the overlap is made. It is quite easy for a boat ahead to luff at the last moment and break the overlap by swinging their transom line around.
- Lining up to do mark traps. If a boat is going to stop at the end of the reach to make use of the mark they will do better if they make sure the position they stop in really does give them control over the mark. The boat needs to line up in the two length zone so that if a boat tries to go inside the gap can be closed quickly enough to stop them going through. The position also needs to allow defence of any boats going around the outside. A useful tip to make this mark trap easier is not to arrive at the mark too early (more of this later).

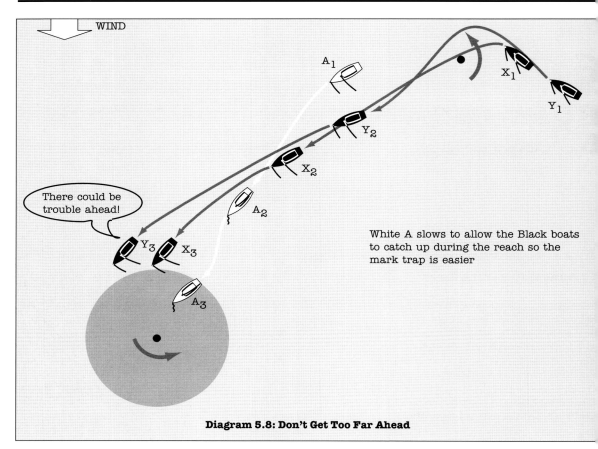

WIND

A₁

X₁

Y₁

Y₂

X₂

A₂

There could be
trouble ahead!

Y₃ X₃

A₃

White A slows to allow the Black boats
to catch up during the reach so the
mark trap is easier

Diagram 5.8: Don't Get Too Far Ahead

Avoiding mark pile ups is advantageous but this becomes very difficult when the reach is broad, creating a big windshadow at the mark. The congestion is made worse because the route around the outside is very slow due to the disturbed air. If behind, one option is to slow early and wait for the boats ahead to either stop completely or for a gap to appear at the mark. Once the boats ahead are committed you can make your move.

TOP TIPS: Reaching

1. Sail to get an overlap at the next mark so you will be on the inside
2. If behind and you are working with a team mate use the high/low method
3. If behind and working alone avoid overlaps with the boat in front and attack the enemy astern
4. If in the lead try not to get too far ahead, otherwise it is hard to attack when needed

6

RUNNING MANOEUVRES

6.1 BASIC RUNNING MANOEUVRES

The run is an enormously interesting leg of a team race. It is possible to make gains and losses by deviating from the straight-line route. In some boats, for example those with asymmetric spinnakers, the straight line route is not even an option, as gybing downwind is needed to keep up the speed to achieve "velocity made good" to the bottom mark. In addition you have the complexity that the boats behind are able to slow the boats in front so the fleet naturally tends to get squashed up. Added to that the leg begins and ends with some difficult mark roundings. **Don't relax on the run!**

6.1.1 Keeping a lead – Diagram 6.1

If we first assume the boats are quite far apart so that there is no imminent danger of overtaking, then it is appropriate if ahead to try and stay ahead. The boat behind will start to cover the lead boats in an attempt to slow them from astern using her windshadow. As windshifts go through and gusts arrive it will be important to use them to advantage. Whereas in upwind trailing the boat behind tacks and the one ahead **follows** to cover this method is more risky for the lead boat on a run. The lead boat is well advised to "cover", or protect their position, by **responding first** to shifts and gusts so that the air is kept clearer. Alternatively the lead boat can sail a parallel but offset course and only come across onto the tailing boat's track at the end of the leg when there is no risk of giving away an overlap. This is the equivalent of the upwind remote cover.

6.1.2 The Flier – Sailing off to one side of the run

This is when a boat takes an 'off the rhumb line' route down the run. Often the clear air (and wind direction or strength advantage) will result in a gain. The lighter and more fickle the breeze or the longer the run the more effective it may be. The usual defence by the

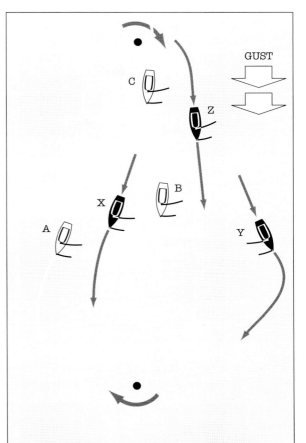

Black had 2nd, 3rd & 5th at the start of the leg (WIN)

❍ Black Y has taken a flyer and might get 1st with the gust on her side

❍ The boats have spread to avoid slowing in wind shadows

❍ Black X is well placed to make gybing a problem for White A

❍ Black Z can luff or gybe or sail on as it wishes and has control over White C

❍ White C has unfortunately got into a position where its wind shadow will affect White B

Diagram 6.1: Running – Keeping a Lead

leading team is to spread out across the course but this in itself inevitably means some overtaking will occur as gusts will not be spread consistently. The flier is a fundamental way of using leverage to overtake your opponents.

RUNNING, the basic guidelines are:
If ahead: Do what you would do in a fleet race, including keeping your wind clear
If behind: Try using your windshadow to slow those ahead
In either case: Always react more quickly than the opposition to shifts and gusts to gain the advantage
Good boatspeed and good gybes will help your cause and keep your options open far longer.

From behind, the evasive tactics of the leaders should mean you find them difficult to catch. The windshadow technique is still worth using even many lengths away.

6.1.3 Running Overlaps – Diagram 6.2

If a boat, previously clear ahead, gets an opposition boat overlapped to windward from astern then she can employ luffing manoeuvres as on a reach. Refer to the reaching section for the principles. The key differences with running are:

- ❍ The overlap can happen very quickly due to the strong windshadow effect slowing the boat ahead.
- ❍ The proper course of any boats involved is more vague since a wide range of proper course can be justified on a running leg.
- ❍ The boats can change tack more easily by gybing, so creating new instantaneous overlap opportunities.
- ❍ The impact of a big luff is to drastically slow the progress of the boats involved – they can end up head to wind – not so much "slowing" as stopping!

TOP TIPS: Basic running
- ❍ Identify which is the favoured side of the course
- ❍ Know whether you will lose or gain speed when you gybe
- ❍ Plan your run so that you can get on the inside at the leeward mark
- ❍ Beware of going to windward of opposition boats because a luff can be very costly in distance lost. Being head to wind is a slow way of getting down the run!!

6.2 ADVANCED RUNNING MANOEUVRES

I have classified the largest portion of downwind manoeuvring as "advanced". The transitions are more rapid than on the upwind leg due to the instantaneous nature of a gybe. Things get hectic!

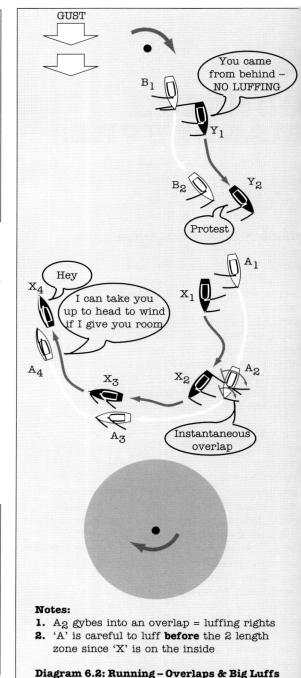

Notes:
1. A_2 gybes into an overlap = luffing rights
2. 'A' is careful to luff **before** the 2 length zone since 'X' is on the inside

Diagram 6.2: Running – Overlaps & Big Luffs

6.2.1 Close cover – Diagrams 6.3 & 6.4

As the boats close up on a run the primary method of attacking a boat in front is now to blanket their sails using the running windshadow skills.

As the lead boat tries to avoid being slowed too

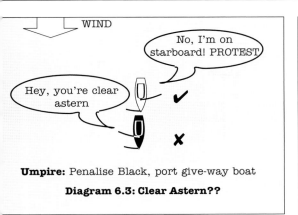

Umpire: Penalise Black, port give-way boat

Diagram 6.3: Clear Astern??

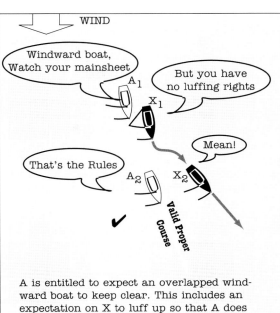

A is entitled to expect an overlapped wind-ward boat to keep clear. This includes an expectation on X to luff up so that A does not run into its mainsheet or boom. As ever, A must give X room to keep clear, but X MUST LUFF as soon as an overlap is ESTABLISHED

Diagram 6.4: New windward boat MUST keep clear

much it may try sailing high, or sailing low or gybing. If the boats are still not overlapped the boat behind will try and match these moves in order to stay directly upwind of the opponent and therefore get ever closer.

A boat behind can catch up very quickly and is therefore wise to be aware of Rule 12, **On The Same Tack, Not Overlapped** which says that when boats are on the same tack and not overlapped, a boat clear astern shall keep clear of a boat clear ahead. It is important to be constantly aware of a situation involving running boats which are not on the same tack. I have frequently seen experienced sailors caught out by thinking they are clear ahead when in fact they are ahead but are on **port** and therefore have to give way to a **starboard** boat which might run into their transom (Diagram 6.3).

If a boat behind runs into a leeward overlap situation with the boat ahead there is a transition as the boats are now subject to Rule 11, **On The Same Tack, Overlapped** which requires the windward boat to keep clear. In order to keep clear it may be necessary to expect the windward boat to sail to windward to get clear. This is not considered or allowed to be a "luff" since the leeward boat is restricted by Rule 17.1, **On The Same Tack; Proper Course** because the overlap has been gained from clear astern. Nevertheless the **windward boat** has to (and is expected to) 'luff' to remain clear of a leeward boat that is on its proper course.

The boat coming in from behind is not allowed to run straight into the mainsheet of the other boat as it has **acquired** right of way and is therefore obliged to allow response time for the new give-way boat (Diagram 6.4). The leeward boat may even be able to justify some alteration of course to windward in order to assume a legitimate proper course. This is because the proper course is:

> **"any course a boat might take to finish as soon as possible in the absence of other boats".**

Since the run often features widely differing angles and courses, all aiming to get boats to the same leeward mark objective, boats can justify some "proper course" deviation, much more than an umpire would permit on a reach where the straight line route is more often the fastest angle.

6.2.2 Close Cover – The Gybing Duel

As the boats are close together a gybing duel is common. This is a test of gybing skill with both boats trying to gain distance and also to get an opportunity to trap their opponent by gybing onto starboard in a way that pins them out, i.e., in their control zone. Once the boats are about to become overlapped it is absolutely critical to manage how the boats come together such that you control the situation.

- ⭕ Control means you want to be the boat gybing onto starboard towards the other boat or you want to be leeward and on the same tack.
- ⭕ Since both boats may be doing hurried gybes you should note the precise nature of a "gybe". It is important to realise that the gybe takes place as soon as the boat has changed its windward side. The windward side is defined as opposite to the leeward side. The leeward side is defined as away from the wind and in addition, when sailing by the lee or directly downwind, her leeward side is

the side on which **her mainsail lies**. Being even more legalistic about the definitions you need to think about what a reasonable interpretation of "lies" is because this will become relevant when the boom and sail are being deliberately forced across or held on one side to prevent or create a gybe.

The common sense view is that if the leech of the sail looks like it wants to be on the other side of the boat then it would naturally lie on that side so you are already on that gybe. It is not necessarily "the moment it crosses the centreline".

○ The gybe is an instantaneous change of tack. It is not possible to "gybe in someone's water" but it is possible to assume a new tack without having sufficient regard for Rule 15, **Acquiring Right of Way**. The point is you then need to give any boat who becomes the give-way boat as a result of your actions sufficient room to keep clear. If they cannot avoid colliding with you then you may have broken Rule 15.

> **Top Tip:**
> After you gybe on to starboard there must be adequate space and time for a port-tack boat to keep clear by responding promptly in a seamanlike manner

6.2.3 Trap to starboard from astern –
Diagram 6.5

We have identified in the skills section that there is a control zone on the run. When the boats are on starboard the control zone is big since even if the boat can gybe to cross the boat to leeward the starboard boat can alter course to try and prevent the port boat crossing.

The starboard boat needs to comply with Rule 16.2, **Changing Course**. This means that if the port boat is close and just about to cross ahead or behind the starboard boat then the right-of-way

> "starboard boat shall not change course if as a result the port-tack boat would immediately need to change course to continue keeping clear".

To implement this **starboard tack** trap you sail down the left side of the boat in front of you making sure you get onto starboard soon enough to prevent the luff by the port boat. Once on the left side of the other boat you can remain in that position. If the other boat was initially on port then it should gybe before an overlap exists because otherwise it risks fouling under Rule 10, **On Opposite Tacks** (Diagram 6.5).

6.2.4 The port luff – Diagram 6.6
The windward boat which has been trapped by the

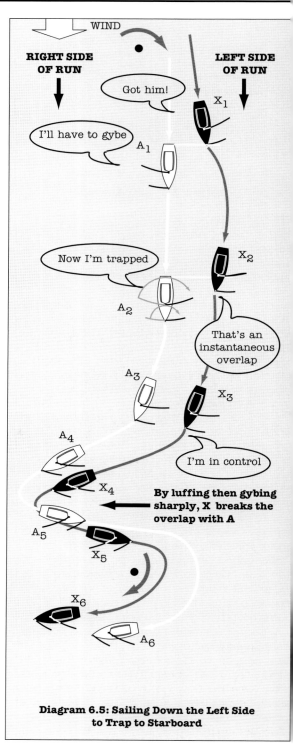

Diagram 6.5: Sailing Down the Left Side to Trap to Starboard

left-side attacker can attempt some defence tactics.
The first of these is to stop the boat passing down

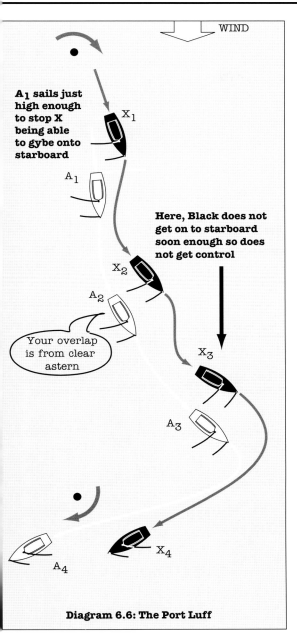

Diagram 6.6: The Port Luff

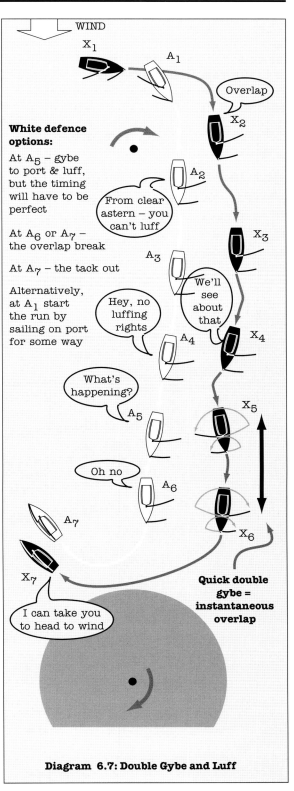

Diagram 6.7: Double Gybe and Luff

the left side by luffing up on port. If the boat crosses the transom of the leading boat on port then the leading boat should immediately get onto port and luff as this will prevent the boat coming from behind getting onto starboard.

6.2.5 Double gybe and luff – Diagram 6.7
To really make use of the trap to the right the left hand boat needs to acquire luffing rights. If both boats have always been on the same tack since the overlap

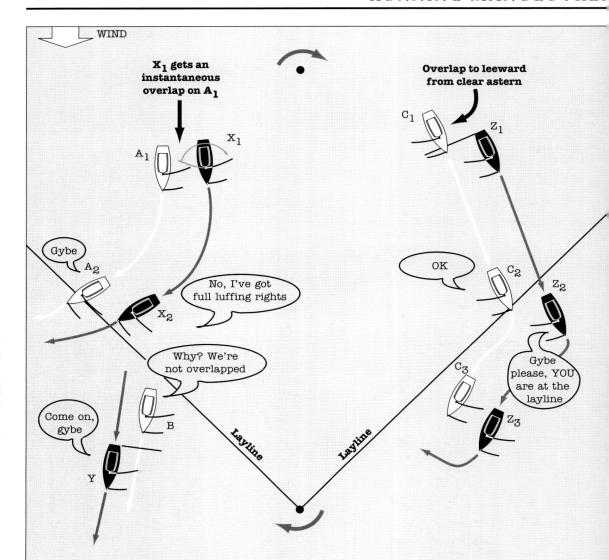

Y could create an overlap, and hence an obligation on B to gybe, by bearing away and slowing

C has to gybe only when it reaches the layline and not when Z reaches it. In this situation Z_3 could now luff C_3 away from the mark

Note: The boat on the right in each pair (as you look at the page) is advantaged in most situations

Diagram 6.8: Sail Beyond the Layline

started then the overlap has been gained from clear astern and the leeward boat can only come up to a proper course. The leeward boat should try to improve its situation by creating an instantaneous overlap. This is done by gybing twice. The fresh overlap created gives luffing rights to head to wind for as long as the

overlap exists. Diagram 6.7 shows the manoeuvre and summarises some of the defence options available.

6.2.6 Breaking the overlap – see Diagram 5.7
As on a reaching leg, a boat trapped to windward can change the status of the overlap by breaking it and

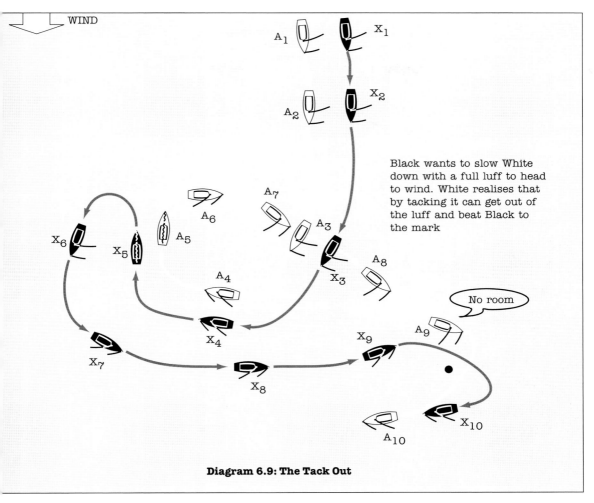

Black wants to slow White down with a full luff to head to wind. White realises that by tacking it can get out of the luff and beat Black to the mark

No room

Diagram 6.9: The Tack Out

getting it to be re-established from astern. The change in overlap type will prevent the leeward boat from being able to stop the windward boat by luffing head to wind. See Diagram 5.7.

6.2.7 Sailing beyond the Layline – Diagram 6.8
If a leeward boat can trap a boat to windward on the run the likely intention is that it will force the windward boat to sail further than it would wish. The run has laylines to the leeward mark. (These are the lines which a boat sailing a proper course would normally, in the absence of other boats, turn at to proceed as fast as possible to the mark.) By sailing an opponent beyond them you will delay their progress.

The definition of proper course, in conjunction with Rule 17.1, **On The Same Tack; Proper Course,** prevents a leeward boat from carrying a windward boat beyond the layline if the overlap was gained from astern. If the overlap does not permit the leeward boat

to luff then when it reaches its layline then the boat must gybe (Boat 'C' in Diagram 6.8). The converse to this is that if the leeward boat does have luffing rights it can carry on forever (until they get to the shore? – X could do this in Diagram 6.8). This might include going past the leeward mark (but without risking going within the two length zone) and then beating back up to it!

If the boats are not overlapped but the boat behind is still in the control zone (on starboard) it may prevent the boat ahead from gybing, if close enough. In this situation there is no obligation on the boat behind to gybe, even when the layline is reached, because there is no application of Rule 17, **On The Same Tack Proper Course,** which affects a boat clear astern. The defence of the "non-overlap hold" is for the boat ahead to create an overlap by bearing away or slowing down (Y could do this by pulling in its mainsail in Diagram 6.8). The turn must not go too far or it will

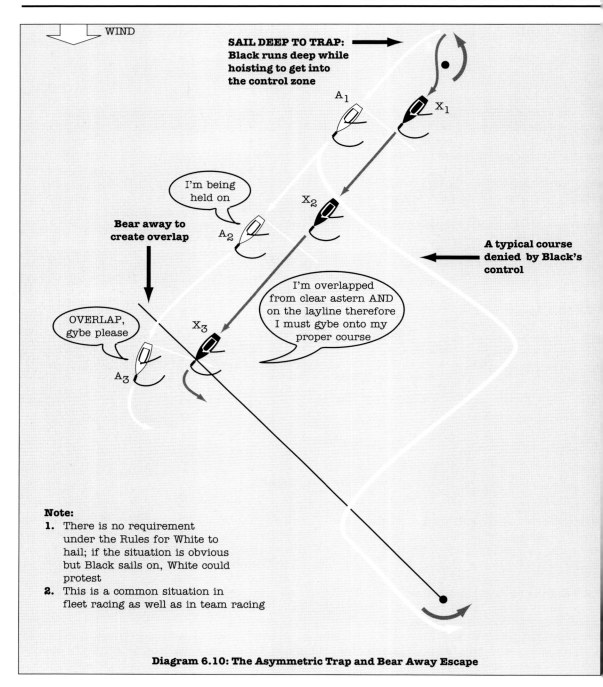

Diagram 6.10: The Asymmetric Trap and Bear Away Escape

be illegal under Rule 17.2 because the boat ahead can only bear down to its proper course and even then only if this does not, in creating an overlap, also create an incident as the turning boat becomes overlapped to windward and is obliged to keep clear. There is no need to hail the illegal 'luffer' to gybe, just protest once well past the layline! – see A3 in Diagram 6.10.

6.2.8 The tack out – Diagram 6.9

The tack out is worth doing if the luffed windward boat cannot escape any other way and if the most important thing for the team is to continue around the course as quickly as possible. The boat simply takes the long way round, coming out heading towards the leeward mark. This is a particularly good option if the leeward boat has got full luffing rights and has taken the boats up to a high course. The windward, attacked boat is likely to lose a lot less than getting involved in an extended luff where it has little prospect of ever breaking through.

All the above manoeuvres describe situations for the lead boat to attack or the boat behind to try and overtake. If the objective of either boat is simply **to slow the pair down** for the benefit of developing the race position then the manoeuvres are still applicable. The safest way of slowing down on the run is to perform the starboard side trap and hold the situation for as long as possible. It is quite normal for a trailing boat to want to slow the game down by deliberately enticing a leading boat to get involved in a long luff. The focus and aggression required to carry out luffs on the run make it likely that a less experienced sailor may lose sight of the overall race situation and continue the luff for too long, allowing other boats to go through.

6.2.9 The Asymmetric Trap

In asymmetric boats such as Melges, which have been used for the British American Cup four boat team race event, there is a particularly frequent situation which arises on the run (Diagram 6.10).

A boat which trails another around the windward mark can carry out a very effective starboard trap. The control zone for a spinnakered boat (particularly asymmetrics) is much bigger because the boat slows in the gybe and has to turn through a greater angle.

The boat behind therefore sails deep out of the mark and is then able to resume a course on the leeward hip of the opponent. Even with several boat lengths between the boats this technique will give the boat behind control of the situation. This technique is powerful and if team racing in asymmetric boats you should aim to leave the windward mark sailing deep. If you are in the lead it may be best to gybe off as soon as possible to avoid the situation developing further down the leg.

TOP TIPS: Advanced running
- ○ Protect the left (as you look down the run) and attack boats by sailing them to the right (your starboard side)
- ○ Use the long luff to compress the race
- ○ Get full luffing rights by doing two quick gybes
- ○ If ahead, use fleet race tactics to stay ahead

7

MARK ROUNDING MANOEUVRES

7.1 KEY MARK ROUNDING OBJECTIVES

If you need to attack other boats aggressively it is often best to attempt the manoeuvre at a mark. The rules, and in particular Rule 18, give more potency to a mark stopping manoeuvre if a serious boat-on-boat encounter is what you require because you need to convert the combination in order to win.

The 'mark-trap' is the name given to the technique of a lead boat stopping or slowing within the vicinity of a mark. It is the aspect of team racing which most differs from other types of sailing. Occasionally it can pay to slow down before a mark in a fleet race, for example when you need to severely slow the progress of a specific opponent at the end of a series. In match racing it can pay to stop at marks as a way of trying to give an opponent a penalty.

The objectives of the mark trap are:

1. Gain an advantage by allowing boats in your team to catch up.
2. Compress the race, or a section of it, even more sharply than is normally possible, by dramatically slowing the progress of boats caught up in the trap.
3. Carry out the mark trap with minimal risk of losing your own race position.
4. Carry out the mark trap with minimal risk of fouling another boat because you have some specific "rule advantages".

Tip: You need significant place changes to win!

YES .... Consider a Mark Trap

NO .... Develop the situation on a leg

If YES but there are no marks left   Good Luck!

7.1.1 Mark 'Rules' – Diagrams 7.1 & 7.2
Rule 18 – Rounding and Passing Marks & Obstruction. This Rule is worded quite briefly and involves some complex interactions of the Rules. There are many type of mark rounding so a lot of different things can happen. We only have a certain amount of mental capacity in our heads so we need to have rules to guide our actions. I have put my version of these below.

Basic Rules of Thumb for Marks
1. Give boats **inside** you **room** to go around.
2. If they got there first and are right of way, **keep clear** of them.
3. At **windward marks** on opposite tacks **take the mark away** (in your mind) and therefore 'normal' rules apply.
4. **Do not barge in late** if you were behind or outside at 2 lengths.
5. **Do not tack just in front** of people at windward marks.
6. If you are clear-ahead or right-of-way boat you can **sail wide** of the mark whilst you **stay clear ahead and/or right of way**. Other boats have to keep clear but your **team mates could go through** and round.
7. If you are **inside** boat **with room** but are give-way you can slow your speed but **must go around** the mark in terms of the course you follow.
8. If you are a leeward boat and have the **right to luff** you can **sail on** at a gybe mark.

See Diagram 7.1.

More Advanced Notes Relating to Applications of Rule 18, Rounding and Passing Marks & Obstructions The relevant Rules are included in brackets, read them
1. You cannot call for room at a **starting** mark this includes the Committee Boat and its lines (Rule 18.1.a).
2. You cannot call for room when on opposite tacks at a windward mark. Boats that are beating on opposite tacks are not considered overlapped. At a downwind mark opposite tack boats **are** considered to be overlapped, and in reality their headings will be similar so this is appropriate (Rule 18.2.a + definitions; overlap).
3. Fundamentally a boat on the **inside needs room** to round the mark. Only having 'Room' means the boat having it doing a normal seamanlike rounding on the correct side of the mark (Rule 18.2.a).
   a. But no 'Room' if a boat 'barged' into a **late overlap** from having been clear-astern (Rule 18.2.b) or was originally outside boat at 2 lengths (Rule 18.2.c). There is an onus on a boat claiming an overlap to have proved it. The

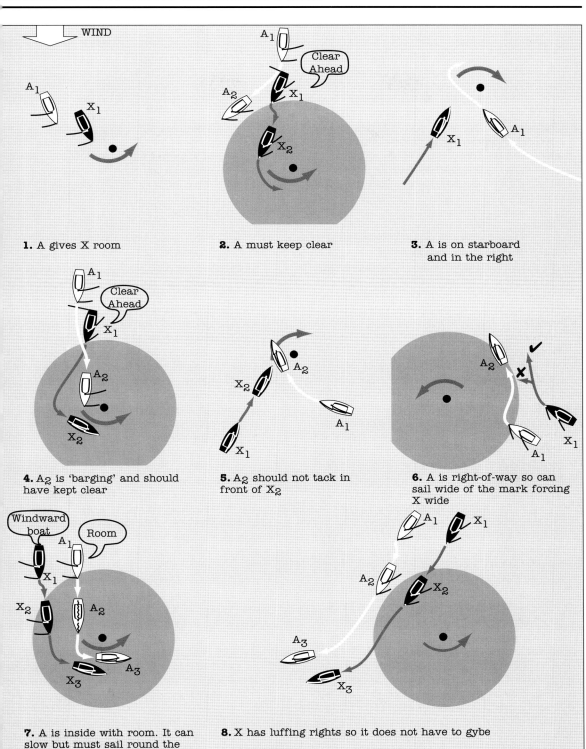

1. A gives X room

2. A must keep clear

3. A is on starboard and in the right

4. A₂ is 'barging' and should have kept clear

5. A₂ should not tack in front of X₂

6. A is right-of-way so can sail wide of the mark forcing X wide

7. A is inside with room. It can slow but must sail round the mark to the next mark

8. X has luffing rights so it does not have to gybe

Diagram 7.1: Marks – Rules of Thumb

umpire will go back to the last facts they were certain of.

b. Also no 'Room' if the outside boat **cannot give room** because of restrictions. For example, the boat inside tacked into a non-existent gap or the **conditions** do not permit space to be given in a seamanlike way (Rule 18.2.e).

4. If a boat has room and is **give-way boat** or becomes give-way boat (e.g., windward boat or port boat) then it **only has room** so must proceed to round the mark without sailing beyond it or wide of it. The boat can actively slow down (by using the sails) but its course (heading) must be consistent with a seamanlike rounding (Rule 18.2.a: Interpretation).

5. But if the inside boat in addition has **right of way** then it has **more power**. It can get right-of-way status by arriving at the mark **clear-ahead** (Rule 18.2.c) or by being inside boat AND having normal right-of-way status generated by leeward overlap or starboard tack. The boat with this power can turn away from the mark, whilst remaining within the 2 length zone and therefore still being considered to be 'about to round or pass the mark'. The boat can effectively stop; **forcing other boats around the outside** (Rule 18.2.a: Interpretation of Keep Clear) **as long as it remains right-of-way boat**.

6. If having stopped, the right-of-way boat creates **a tempting gap** between it and the mark, a boat might try to go into it. If this is a team mate the right-of-way boat will no doubt let them through. If the boat going for the gap is an opposition give-way boat then the outside right-of-way boat will try and **'shut the gap'** and this alteration of course towards the mark is **not** constrained by Rule 16, **Changing Course**. It can **alter course rapidly** providing it does not cause damage under Rule 14, **Avoiding Contact**. Tactically this will then either give the opponent a penalty, or if they spot the gap shutting early enough, it will force a hurried change of plan and the need for the 'barging' boat to head up to go around the outside or miss the mark altogether and spin around to approach a little later (Rule 18.2.d).

7. If one boat needs to do its **last tack** of the beat, to fetch the mark and it completes (gets close-hauled) this tack **within the 2 length zone** it needs to **avoid obstructing any boat** coming in which is also **fetching** (going round without tacking/laying) the mark. Tacking to round the mark effectively makes you give-way boat to any boat coming in which does not need to tack to get round the mark (Rule 18.3).

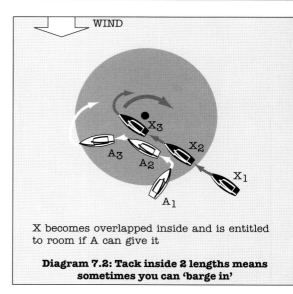

X becomes overlapped inside and is entitled to room if A can give it

Diagram 7.2: Tack inside 2 lengths means sometimes you can 'barge in'

8. **"Barging Sometimes Works"**
Because the fundamental situation at marks is that the **inside boat has room**, if the exceptions (Rules 18.2.b&c) do not apply then there is a different scenario to consider. In those situations where **a boat tacks on to the same tack as another within the zone**, and **both have to tack again** to round the mark. Consider a port tack boat that tacks onto starboard, inside the zone at the starboard-hand windward mark, close to windward or leeward of an incoming starboard tack boat. Under the old rules this was not covered by any of Rule 18, and there was an unofficial 'call' to cover this. Now this situation is addressed by Rule 18.2.a, as neither exception (b) or (c) applies and so the **outside boat has to give the inside boat room** providing she is **able to** (Rule 18.2.e). See Diagram 7.2.

Key Points in Diagram 7.2 are:
❑ As opposite tack boat, Black X was neither 'clear-astern' nor 'outside boat'.
❑ White A's tack is not subject to Rule 18.3 **Tacking** as it has to tack again later.
❑ Black X gains an inside overlap within the zone having not previously had any 'overlap'.
❑ Black X can only have room if White A is able to give it.

9. In the Team Racing Appendix D1.1(b) Rule 18.4, **Gybing** is deleted. This means that if a boat **has luffing rights** and is inside boat it does not need to go around a mark but **can sail on**. It does not need to assume a proper course to the

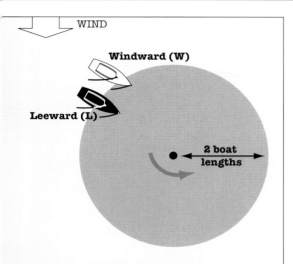

Rule 11 – On the Same Tack – Overlapped
Rule 18 – Passing Marks & Obstructions:
Giving Room; Keeping Clear

QUESTION:
L and W are overlapped, broad reaching on
port tack towards a **leeward mark** which is
to be left to port. The boats are half a length
apart. The **overlap** was established in such a
way that L is not subject to Rule 17.1 (and
therefore may luff). L is steering a course
approximately one length to windward of
the **mark**. Must L bear away or gybe at
the **two-length zone** to provide **room** for
W to round the **mark**?

ANSWER:
Yes. Although L may wish to sail above the
mark, these boats are now "about to pass a
mark". Therefore Rule 18 applies, and L
must comply with Rule 18.2(a) and give W
room to sail a seamanlike course round the
mark from this point.

Diagram 7.3: "About to Pass"

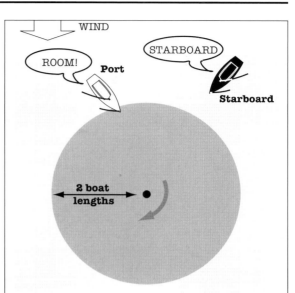

Rule 10 – On Opposite Tacks
Rule 18 – Passing Marks & Obstructions:
When Rule 18 Applies

QUESTION:
Boats P and S are on converging courses
approaching a starboard-hand **leeward mark**.
At what point are they about to pass the
mark so that Rule 18 starts to apply?

ANSWER:
When the leading boat's bow is within the
two-length zone of the **mark** the boats should
definitely be considered to be about to pass it,
and in most circumstances two lengths is an
acceptable measure of "about to pass". In
windy conditions or in big fleets, boats may
need to start to prepare to pass the **mark**
when further from the **mark**; in such cases,
they become "about to pass" when they need
to start preparing to pass the mark.

RULING:
If the boats are within the **two-length zone**
(and not sailing away from the **mark**), they
are "about to pass" the **mark**. In windy
weather or big fleets, they may be "about to
pass" when further than two lengths from
the **mark**.

Diagram 7.4: "About to Pass"

next mark if it is protected or given power by Rule
17.1, **On the Same Tack; Proper Course**, or
indeed Rule 10, **Opposite Tacks**.

0. The whole of Rule 18 applies when boats are 'about
   to round or pass'. Normally this is assumed to be
   when boats are **within 2 lengths of the mark**.
   In extreme conditions it would be further in order
   to allow for a seamanlike rounding by boats with
   room (Diagrams 7.3 & 7.4).

1. Rule 18 stops applying when all boats involved
   have passed the mark. If a mark is no longer
   relevant to the boat's proper course to the
   next mark, it has passed the mark and it cannot

then 'use' Rule 18.

12. As long as a boat is still rounding a mark, not
    passed it, and it is **entitled to room** as inside boat,
    this room includes **enough space to tack or gybe**
    providing to do so is part of the normal rounding.

1.
White is GIVE WAY and on the inside of the two boat length zone with ROOM. The mark is a leeward port hand mark

2.
Round "promptly" means "turn promptly" but not "sail quickly"

Note: Black X_2 should have gone wide and rounded the mark behind, not overlapped on White

Diagram 7.5: Having ROOM

13. If Rule 18 is 'in conflict' with normal right-of-way rules (Rules Part A), or general limitations (Rules Part B), then Part C (Marks) has precedence. As you can see from the above notes the exact way this precedent operates is complex and is best summarised by the following box (on page 99)…

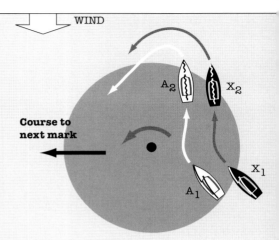

1. Outside give way boat keeps clear
White has right of way & Black must keep clear, so White slows the mark rounding significantly

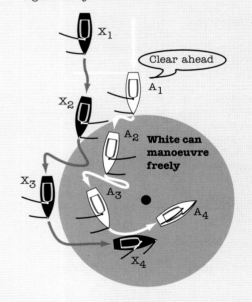

2. White A_1 is CLEAR AHEAD as it enters the two length zone. White manoeuvres freely (only constrained by Rule 16) slowing the mark rounding significantly

Black X_3 gybes and White A_3 chooses to gybe to windward so becoming give way boat. Black now gives ROOM and White must go round the mark otherwise she would be sailing below her proper course & bearing down on Black outside her

Diagram 7.6: Keeping Clear, Having ROOM

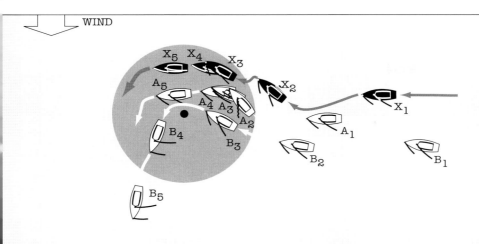

White A luffs at the start of the two length zone slowing Black X and allowing White B inside. White A then starts sailing fast again in time to avoid the threat of starting sailing down the run slowly

Diagram 7.7: Stopping Safely – Effective Mark Traps

Mark Rules use right of way, room and obligations to police what goes on at marks...

1. Does Rule 18 establish a **right of way**?
   If Yes → It can be used to override normal rules
   If NO → See 2
2. Does Rule 18 offer protection of **room** to a boat?
   If YES → Then Rule 18 provides some defence against normal rules adequate to permit your rounding
   If NO → Then you have no room and therefore Rule 18 does not help you, in fact it requires you to avoid others
3. Do any of the **obligations** listed in the Rule apply at any time?
   If YES → Then they override the normal rules by adding or removing a burden on you

7.2 BASIC MARK MANOEUVERING

7.2.1 Stopping in the two length zone

Diagrams 7.5, 7.6 & 7.7

The "rule advantages" referred to in point 7.11 above relate to the additional protection of Rule 18, Passing Marks and Obstructions. Any boat getting to a two boat length zone overlapped on the **outside** of another boat must **give** the inside boat ROOM. Any boat getting to the two length zone **clear astern** must KEEP CLEAR of the boat ahead.

Only having ROOM is slightly less powerful than other boats having to KEEP CLEAR.

ROOM implies the inside boat should manoeuvre promptly in a seamanlike way. This is interpreted as going around the mark on a course near to the mark. It does not mean the inside boat has to go fast. It can slow on its course to the mark, thus forcing boats outside to take the long route or try and accelerate around the outside (see Diagram 7.5).

If the inside boat has right of way under Rules other than 18 then it can exert its rights by luffing (as leeward boat) or altering course (as starboard boat). If a boat is inside and has right of way then it can manoeuvre with conviction to expect the outside boat to KEEP CLEAR. This can include deviating off the direct route around the mark and sailing to the edge of the zone and beyond (Diagram 7.6(1)).

If a boat arrives at the two length zone clear ahead then she can also slow and deviate from the direct route round the mark. She can only do this as long as she holds right of way. As soon as a boat becomes right of way over her, by for example getting a leeward overlap on the outside, then the inside boat becomes obliged to manoeuvre promptly in a seamanlike way (to pass the mark). So other boats will KEEP CLEAR but if they **subsequently** get right of way then the inside boat changes to only having ROOM.

It is an important skill to realise that stopping **effectively** involves accelerating again at the right time. Diagram 7.7 illustrates this. Even if you have the right to remain stopped there is a moment when you will have maximised the gains for the minimum of risk.

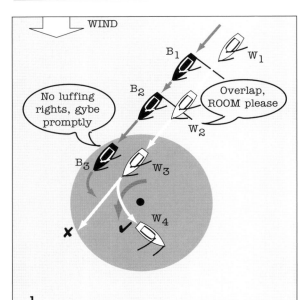

1.
White CANNOT do the sail past here because there are no luffing rights

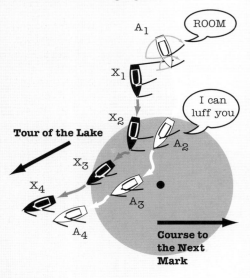

Tour of the Lake

Course to the Next Mark

2.
White gybes into an abeam overlap with luffing rights before the two length zone.
NOTE: This differs from fleet racing because Appendix D changes Rule 18.4 (Gybing at a Mark)

Diagram 7.8: The Sail Past the Mark

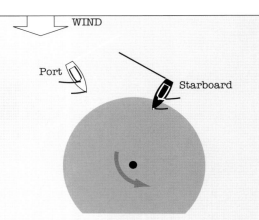

Rule 18 – Passing Marks & Obstructions:
Gybing
Rule D1.1(b) – Deletion of Rule 18.4

QUESTION:
Boats P and S are on converging courses approaching a port-hand leeward **mark**. Does S have to gybe and round the **mark**?

ANSWER:
No! As boats on opposite tacks may only be considered to be **overlapped** when Rule 18 applies, any **overlap** that exists, does so only when the leading boat reaches the **two length zone**.

When S reaches the **two-length zone**, S and P become **overlapped** for the purposes of the rules. As neither is **clear astern**, the **overlap** is "instantaneous".

As the boats are **overlapped** Rule 18.2(a) applies. While S's **proper course** is to gybe at the **mark**, D1.1(b) deletes Rule 18.4, Gybing. Therefore S does not have to gybe at the **mark**, and may instead sail on.

Diagram 7.9: Sail Past The Mark

You should start sailing fast again when…

1. The rules concerning passing marks cease to protect you and you become **past** the mark (assuming you're not right-of-way).
2. The risk of remaining stopped is too high. This is exacerbated by loss of steerage-way.
3. Your position is beginning to be threatened by opposition boats which have gone around the outside of the bunch.
4. Your assessment of 'minding the gaps' means that you have done enough to compress the race.

7.2.2 The sail past the mark –
Diagrams 7.8 & 7.9
If a boat is inside and right-of-way then it is able to continue the "trap" beyond the mark. As right-of-way boat it can force the give-way boat past the mark and make it continue in the wrong direction. The extent to

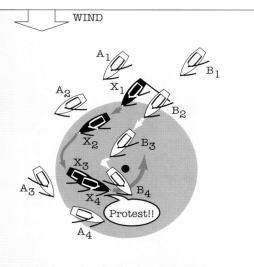

Black slows inside the two length zone having made it clear that White B has no room at position 1. White B is dead! White B tries to go for the gap and is trapped by Black who is then careful not to cause damage

Diagram 7.10: The Tempting Gap

mistake. The leading boat can make a gap between the mark and itself and possibly feign a lack of control only to then shut the gap and either collide with an inside boat (being careful to not cause damage) or force it to miss out the mark and go around again. This manoeuvre is all about forcing a big error out of the opposition. You need to know your own boat's manoeuvrability and assess your opponent's. In particular you need to be able, as either boat, to predict the acceleration and turning ability for the conditions you are in.

Tip: Just be careful not to be too aggressive when "shutting the gap" and find you have broken Rule 14, Avoiding Contact.

> **Tip:**
> If you have made a gap then you can, provided you have right of way over any opposition boats, allow any team mates to sail through the gap while you remain stopped

7. 3 ADVANCED MARK ROUNDING MANOEUVRES

Some marks offer better opportunities than others by exposing the stopping boat to fewer rule difficulties because they have the protection of room at the mark. It is important to think about how the boat…

1. Enters the mark rounding (is it easy to slow, is it right-of-way boat?).
2. What transitions the boat goes through during the rounding (e.g. tacking).
3. How will the boat leave the mark (do they have to round up to a beat, is there a difficult gybe?).

> **This means it is risky to stop if:**
> ❏ the rounding involves a tack
> ❏ the rounding involves a turn through 180°
> ❏ the rounding is onto a long run
> ❏ the turn is difficult and the conditions are poor (very light or choppy)
> **It is easier to stop if:**
> ❏ You will remain right-of-way throughout the rounding
> ❏ you do not need to tack during the rounding
> ❏ you are turning onto a reaching course
> ❏ the conditions are good

which the sail past can work is driven by whether the inside boat has the right to luff. If the inside boat had originally gained its overlap from clear astern then it will have to assume a proper course to the next mark. This might include an obligation to gybe at the first reasonable opportunity.

Note that this is different from fleet racing. In fleet racing an inside leeward boat at a gybe mark (which includes leeward marks where gybes are needed to go round) is **always** obliged to proceed around if the outside boat was overlapped on her **at** the two length circle. This is Rule 18.4, **Gybing**. In team racing, Appendix D deletes this rule. **In summary, if you have the right to luff, carry on**.

The sail past can also be made to work where the boats approach each other from opposite tacks. An inside boat which is on starboard can force an outside port boat to gybe and then sail them on past the mark (Diagram 7.9).

7.2.3 The Tempting Gap – Diagram 7.10
A frequently used tactic by a clear-ahead boat is to use the right to manoeuvre freely to sail some way from the mark without risking having passed it. A boat coming in from behind is likely to be interested in going the quick way round the mark rather than waiting for the boat ahead to finish messing around. This can be a big

7.3.1 Upwind Mark Rounding – Key differences from downwind marks
If boats are both on the **same** tack going past a mark then the general principles described above apply. As soon as the boats are on **opposite** tacks, or one or both boats will need to **tack**, the situation is more complicated.

Wilson Trophy 2000 – Port hand windward mark. The Blue team has boats Nº34, 35 & 36, the Yellow team has Nº31, 32 & 33 (Nº31 is out of the shot). Nº33 slows at the mark and stops Nº35. Meanwhile team mate in Nº32 is able to prevent the two other Blue boats (Nº34 & 36) from tacking. Note the control of speed and the positioning. Nº33 = Steve Tylecote & Debs Kershaw and Nº32 = Roger Morris & Jane Stamp

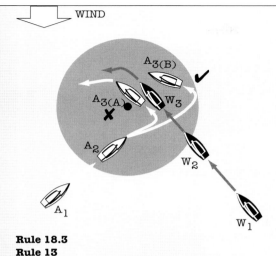

Rule 18.3
Rule 13

White cannot cross safely

At $A_{3(A)}$ White on port must not tack and obstruct Black

At $A_{3(B)}$ White ducks and tacks within the two-length zone and keeps clear of Black and so is OK – a better option

**Diagram 7.11: Port-hand Windward Mark –
Boats on Opposite Tacks**

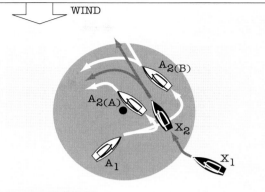

Rules 18.3 & 13
White can cross

In this example White A can cross Black. At $A_{2(A)}$, White tacks on the layline and due to slowing in the tack, illegally obstructs Black.

At $A_{2(B)}$, White has sailed sufficiently far that it will keep clear of Black even though Black gains an inside overlap on it at the mark. Black could sail $A_{2(B)}$ on past the mark if the overlap was established by White's tack

**Diagram 7.12: Port-hand Windward Mark –
Boats on Opposite Tacks**

Upwind marks are subject to a quite different set of rules. The specific rules for marks do not apply if:

◯ the boats are on opposite tacks on a beat to windward. In this case the port/starboard situation overrides and you can effectively 'take the mark away' to determine who is right.

◯ the boats are beating and one of them needs to tack to round the mark. This is excluded from most of Rule 18 so that Rule 13, **While Tacking** applies instead. Effectively you again take the mark away as a boat complies with rules from other sections (see also Rule 18.3).

7.3.2 Windward mark – boats on opposite tacks

Port rounding – Diagrams 7.11 & 7.12

Here the port tack boat is approaching as give-way boat. Assuming the boats are on a collision course the port tack boat will probably have to duck the starboard tacker. If instead it tries to tack near the mark there are some interesting obligations created by the application of Rule 18.3, **Tacking at a Mark**. This rule states that if a boat is on an opposite tack to another and intends to tack within the two length zone then this boat shall…

1. **Not cause the other boat to sail above close hauled or prevent the other boat from passing the mark.**

This means that when White tacks and slows down it may fall foul of Rule 18.3, **Tacking at a Mark**, if the other boat is prevented from rounding the mark. The precise description above refers to forcing a boat above a close-hauled course, so it is sometimes possible to get away with tacking inside if the other boat was already sailing below close hauled, perhaps having overstood the mark, and is therefore not going to need to go above close hauled.

The definition of "prevent the other boat from passing the mark" is not absolutely clear but stopping at the mark to perform a mark trap would not be permissible.

2. **Give room if the other boat (which has not tacked) becomes overlapped inside her.**

If White slows in the tack and Black decides to go below her, White has no rights and must get out of the way. White should cross ahead, sail on for a short distance and tack leaving sufficient room for Black to go inside.

If this is the scenario and the boats proceed past the mark it is important to know whether the boat which became overlapped on the inside has the right to sail on past the mark. This will depend on whether luffing rights were gained as the port tack boat completed its tack by becoming close-hauled. The sequence of events is similar to a slam dunk.

Note that Rule 18.3, **Tacking at a Mark** only applies

WIND

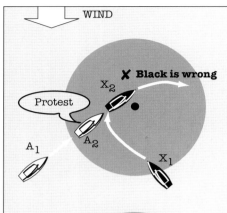

✗ Black is wrong

Protest

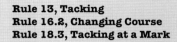

Rule 13, Tacking
Rule 16.2, Changing Course
Rule 18.3, Tacking at a Mark

Black fouls! Despite approaching on starboard it is not allowed to tack and obstruct a boat which has not tacked, or a boat which tacked before it

Some Options are... (1 to 4)

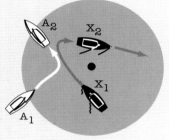

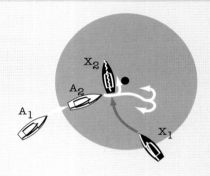

1.
Force a collision course so White has to tack. Black at X₁ regulates its speed to force the port tack White to tack. N.B. Black may not "hunt" due to Rule 16.2, Changing Course

2.
Black forces White to duck but does not tack. White has not got room to go between Black and the mark. White may have to miss out the mark and gybe or tack around

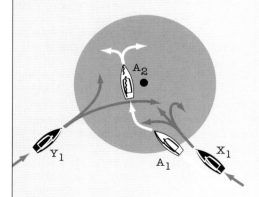

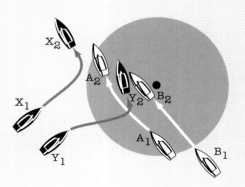

3.
White simply stops at the mark and waits until it is clear to tack. The risk is White losing control and either tacking accidentally or leaving a gap. Either action could foul either X or Y

4.
Here A₂ sails on past the mark, retaining starboard rights and therefore catching X. This also allows B to approach the mark unimpeded and force Y to avoid her

Diagram 7.13: Starboard Rounding – Opposite Tacks

f the other boat is 'fetching' the mark (she won't have o tack).

Top Tip:
○ Plan the last section of your beat to avoid meeting a boat at the mark when you need to tack. Don't tack inside, DUCK

Starboard Rounding – Opposite Tacks, Diagram 7.13
The windward starboard-hand mark rounding is slightly different for boats approaching on opposite tacks because the starboard tack boat will have to tack to round he mark. When tacking the **Passing Marks** rules do not apply, just as before, and so the boat is subject to Rule 13, **While Tacking**. Even if the starboard boat successfully completes a tack onto port then it is subject to the same obligations under Rule 18.3, **Tacking** that the port tack boat was under at a port rounding. This means it cannot complete a tack inside the two length zone and then obstruct a now same-tack boat as it tries to pass the mark.

Obviously the starboard boat approaches the scene as right-of-way boat, but it will have to tack at some stage. The starboard tacker's options are therefore dictated by the relative position of the boats. It could:

1. Force a collision course to make the port boat tack off, and then tack free of the burden of Rule 18.3.
2. Again force a collision course by regulating speed and allow the port tack boat to duck it in such a way that it misses the mark. The port tack boat may slow and try and go for the gap. The starboard tack boat will slow in response and the outcome might be messy. If it is a collision then the port tack boat was give-way and had no rights to room at the mark.

The starboard tacker will try to control the approach as above as a preference, but if all else fails then...

3. The starboard tacker arrives at the mark and luffs to above close hauled and stops until such a time that it can tack legally. By slowing, the starboard boat risks losing control and even tacking accidentally and risking fouling.
4. The starboard tacker has the very safe option of sailing on past the mark. This will allow the port tacker to go through but there might be other boats which will be impeded. At least with this method the starboard boat will not foul. It is a good option when there are boats of your team also coming in on starboard; leave them to do the work if they are going to arrive at the mark at a more suitable moment for your team and a difficult one for your opponents.

7.3.3 Windward marks – stopping boat will not need to tack – Diagrams 7.14 & 7.15
The difficult tactical situations described above mean

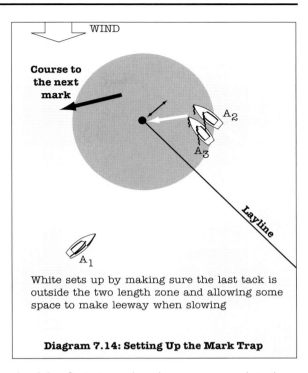

White sets up by making sure the last tack is outside the two length zone and allowing some space to make leeway when slowing

Diagram 7.14: Setting Up the Mark Trap

that it is safer to try and engineer an approach to the mark where you do not have the problem of your last tack being inside the two-length circle. This is easier to achieve where you are doing a port rounding and will therefore remain on starboard throughout. Since both teams will try and do this it is common to see boats rounding on the same tack. If you do need to come in on port it is best to approach just outside the two-length zone making sure your tack is outside the zone. You have then arrived at the mark with normal rights under Rule 18, **Passing Marks** and can block the mark very effectively (see Diagram 7.14).

To execute this manoeuvre effectively the boat anticipates that it will have to stop and "sets up" slightly above the layline. Not too far above the layline or boats will be tempted to sail to tack inside, where they will hope that the starboard boat will not have to sail above close hauled to keep clear of them. Having set up, the boat then remains within the two length zone and prepares to slow any approaching opposition boats by the following methods (assuming a port rounding – Diagram 7.15):

1. If they are approaching on port you make it impossible for them to tack through on the inside because you are close enough to the mark. If they head towards that gap close it by accelerating and taking a course directly to the mark (under Rule 18.3 it will take a big gap for them to get away with it).

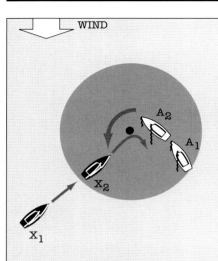

1.
Black tries to go for the gap. White sails on towards the mark enough to prevent this

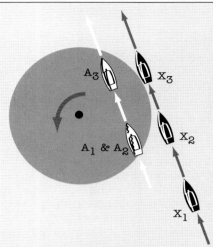

2.
Black tries to go round the outside, White accelerates, with luffing rights and sails Black on

3.
Black tries to go inside. White shuts the gap preventing Black going round the mark

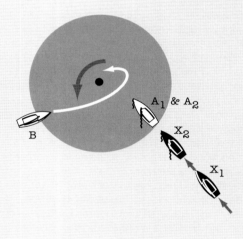

4.
Black stops astern of White. White remains stopped as well, possibly allowing its team mate to go through

Diagram 7.15: Mark Traps – How to 'Block'

2. If they approach on the same tack from clear astern and go to windward of you then luff them. You have the right to luff them to head-to-wind and can also sail them past the mark if they start to overhaul you to windward.

3. If they are on the same tack and go inside they do not have any right to room. You arrived at the mark clear ahead and can bear down to force them to continue to keep clear as long as you have the protection of 'intending to pass the mark'. Do not let them in the gap. You should be careful not to take a course too far off your normal route around the mark so it remains straightforward to 'shut the gap' if the opposition looks like going in it. Beware of sailing below the course to the next mark (Rule 17.3).

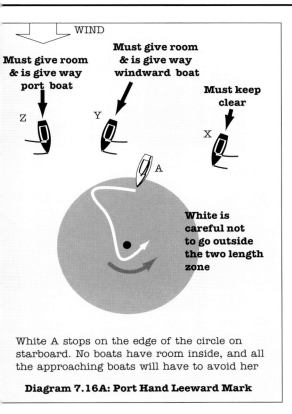

White A stops on the edge of the circle on starboard. No boats have room inside, and all the approaching boats will have to avoid her

Diagram 7.16A: Port Hand Leeward Mark

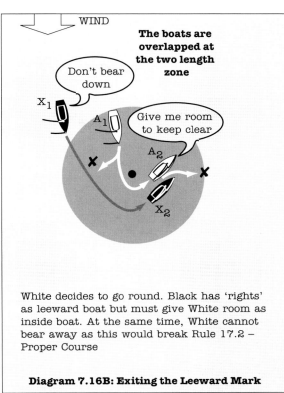

White decides to go round. Black has 'rights' as leeward boat but must give White room as inside boat. At the same time, White cannot bear away as this would break Rule 17.2 – Proper Course

Diagram 7.16B: Exiting the Leeward Mark

.   If the opposition boat stops either on the other tack or on the same tack behind you then you also remain stopped. The large number of safe options make this a very safe way of stalling the race.

If the windward mark is to starboard then the windward mark trap is not so easy. Stopping as port boat is high risk and only possible as long as no starboard boats get involved. If you stop as starboard boat at a starboard windward mark then you will certainly stall the race. You also have the problem of getting moving again and getting in a tack without fouling boats approaching on either tack.

So good is the entertainment that this starboard hand mark and a short reach to the finish was chosen for the Columbus Cup where high spectator appeal was sought for a "prize money" regatta. In any race which was unstable this last mark always proved to be a pivotal moment in the race.

7.3.4 Leeward mark to port

Diagrams 7.16A & 7.16B

To perform a mark trap at a port hand leeward mark it is best to be on the inside, on starboard with luffing rights. As long as you arrived at the mark with the rights you are claiming then all other boats will have to keep clear – Diagram 7.16A. As with the windward mark trap, pro-

tect the gap and stop anyone going inside. If anyone goes to windward, luff them. Be careful that the boat going to windward does not entice you out-side the two-length zone, as you are then are subject to new overlap situations as you approach the mark.

If instead you are on port on the inside (Diagram 7.16B) you are then given room to pass the mark but boats to leeward of you are not expected to tolerate manoeuvres away from the mark. They do not have to tolerate your deviating from a course to round the mark promptly in a seamanlike way. The inside windward boat can sail slowly to cause boats to have to go out-side, but if you get to a point where you are past the mark then you must head up onto the beat.

If in your manoeuvring you turn to head below the mark you must be sure you are not bearing down on a boat overlapped (D1.1(a)). This is an example of rules interacting since Rule 18, **Rounding or Passing Marks** does not conflict with Rule D1.1(a) **On the Same Tack; Proper Course** once you are **not** on a course consistent with rounding the mark, so both rules apply.

If you have slowed at the leeward mark and a boat then comes underneath, on the outside of you, with speed, as you go onto the beat and the 'protection' of 'room' is no longer with you then it must still give you time under Rule 16, **Changing Course**. So if they

World Team Racing Champioships 1995 – Leeward Mark. GBR 2 (Black with boats Nº1, 2 & 3) have gone round this mark a little too bunched together. Boat Nº3 will probably be looking to tack off very soon after getting clear of the mark

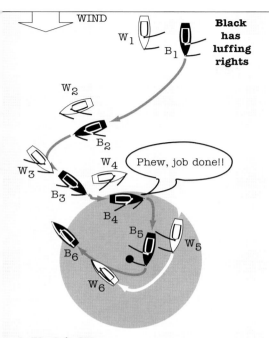

1. Black is OK
Black times the gybe to prevent White getting room inside. Black achieves this by sailing to the top of the two length zone at the end of the leg, rather than the mark itself

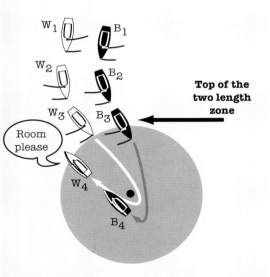

2. Black gets it wrong
Here Black gybes back too early and then sails to the mark and NOT to the top of the two length zone. As a result White is able to get room and goes round the mark in the lead

Diagram 7.17: Leeward Mark to Starboard

come in shouting "windward boat" and hit you as you struggle to get your speed up you are allowed some reasonable time to respond as long as you react once the boats are overlapped. Whether you're obliged to luff above close hauled will depend on how the overlap originally started (does the leeward boat have luffing rights?).

7.3.5 Leeward mark to starboard – Diag 7.17
The approach to the starboard mark is difficult because luffing, on starboard, takes the boats out to the right looking down the run. They are therefore coming back towards the mark on port and will first have to get to the two length zone to gain the rights of an inside boat. The method of achieving control at the rounding is to time the gybe onto port to head back to the mark so that you are going to be clear ahead. Generally this means doing a small luff followed by a skillful gybe and then heading directly to the top of the two length zone. Do not head straight to the mark since this makes it easier for the trailing boat to dive down the inside.

The trailing boat should still avoid getting any unwanted overlaps as it exits the mark, even if it means slowing. If you do go outside the boat ahead of you then you lose the option to tack and then attack any enemy boat astern of you.

> **Tip:**
> Always try to round close to the mark not outside other boats

7.3.6 Stopping at the finish – Diagram 7.18
The finish line has two 'passing marks' at which Rule 18, **Passing Marks and Obstructions** applies. Both ends of the line have a two-length zone.

The easiest way to slow a boat finishing is to do a mark trap manoeuvre to stop a boat which is approaching the finish on or above the layline. As they are forced to go to leeward apply a windshadow on them to slow their progress. Alternatively they might go above you and be forced to tack or gybe around. If this is done correctly you can be certain of finishing in front and the slowing effect might be enough to let one of your team mates get in front. In Diagram 7.18 White B slows Black Y by luffing. Y hails for ROOM in an attempt to get B to stop luffing but B realises that this is an invalid hail (Y is too far from the end of the line to need room) so B can continue luffing thus stopping Y before the finish.

There is plenty of opportunity for special tactics at the finish line. Other manoeuvres to try include:
1. Trapping out to one side with a close cover;
2. Forcing someone to cross the finish line and then staying in the race yourself so you can still assist your team;

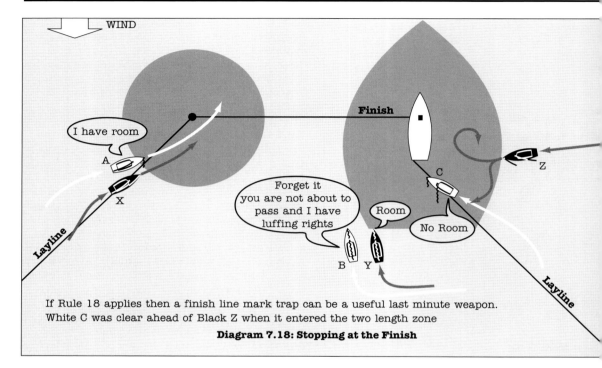

If Rule 18 applies then a finish line mark trap can be a useful last minute weapon. White C was clear ahead of Black Z when it entered the two length zone

Diagram 7.18: Stopping at the Finish

3. Shooting the line: luffing to head-to-wind just before you reach the line when the finish is close.
    Always include finishes in your practices so that you can try these options. Remember: It isn't over until the fat lady sings!

Top Tips: Defending against a mark trap

The following general defences will help you out:

1. Consider attacking an enemy boat astern of you rather than getting tangled up with the opposition boat stopped at the mark in front of you.
2. If you are with a team mate in the combination "split" such that one of you goes around the outside while the other initially stops astern and then subsequently threatens to go in the gap.
3. "Push" a boat on around leeward marks by getting to leeward of them and calling them to go round the mark.
4. At windward mark traps where the stopping boat is on port, approach on starboard.
5. At windward mark traps where you are on the same tack try to overstand the mark so you can sail round the outside without being trapped in a luff.

Top Tips: Mark rounding

❍ When at marks don't forget you have the burden of 'additional obligations', in particular: **Acquiring Right of Way** and **Avoiding Contact**, so don't play it too rough.

❍ Make your overlap status obvious to the boats around you and to the umpires **before** you reach the two-length zone AND when you get to it.

❍ If you need to 'keep clear' of a boat ahead of you try to avoid going outside her unless you are sacrificing yourself to keep the race moving (for instance if the boat behind you is a team mate).

❍ Do not 'go for the gap' unless you believe the risk is worthwhile and the outside boat is not on an intercepting course.

❍ If you only have **room** then keep your rounding **seamanlike**.

❍ If you have the right to expect other boats to **keep clear** then use it, enjoy yourself, this is your chance to show off!

Part III
THE WINNING TEAM

Part III examines the main elements of **working together** as a team. It will help you understand what makes an effective team tick, and how difficult issues like selection, learning and coaching can be approached so they are most likely to be **successful and enjoyable**.

Part III then has a section looking at the specific rule points raised by the **Racing Rules' Team Racing Appendix.**

Part III also has a summary of how to implement tactics with an appreciation of:
1.   **Managing risk** when making team racing decisions, and
2.   How to **use the gaps** between boats to determine your combination strategy (a reminder from Part I).

Four boat team racing is a subset of the sport but is great fun; it is the format used for the **British American Cup**, and hence a section on four boat tactics has been included for your reference. It provides simple rules of thumb which enable you to 'see the race' clearly and concentrate on what matters.

Umpiring is a key part of top level team racing and a section advising both the sailor and the Umpire has been included. There are also sections on specific crewing skills and, with training in mind, coaching children.

Together you can be **A Winning Team**.

Wilson Trophy 2001 – West Kirby. Boat N°11 (Leo Dixon & Katie Parry) are inside Spinnaker 2, N°9 (Dave Ellis & Steve Beresford) at a starboard hand windward mark. N°11 is controlling N°9 who must give room

8

THE WINNING TEAM

8.1 TEAM PREPARATION

8.1.1 Team basics

Never lose sight of the fact that teamwork is the core of success.

- **Teamwork** is the ability to work together towards a common vision.
- In a team **the whole is greater than the sum of the parts**.
- **Attitude** is a little thing that makes a big difference.

The basis of a team may be from a variety of sources. An educational establishment may traditionally have a 1st team, a 2nd team and a Ladies team (not that Ladies need be excluded from the other teams!). There may even be teams for different years or age groups. A sailing club may have a similar arrangement. The mere existence of a team name does not sort out who should be on that team. Here we may come across some ground rules for eligibility which the sponsoring authority may introduce. This may include the person being a member of the relevant establishment. An alternative is to form a 'scratch' team of friends. This option can be harder to sustain due to there not being a convenient group of six available all the time. The establishment, or club, base has a number of benefits:

- It provides a natural geographic focus for the team.
- There will normally be access to some resources such as people to help run racing, a club house, sailing water and even funding and boats.
- The existence of a home venue means the teams can establish a practice base and hence broaden the participation in the sport. Team practice can be available, scheduled and fun. The use of an existing sailing centre provides a promotional opportunity for the sport.
- Having a home team is likely to encourage that club to host an event.

8.1.2 Team dynamics

An understanding of the psychological aspects of a team game and sport in general is essential for top competition where it is pre-supposed that the teams competing will be well-matched. If they are not of equal skill then psychological factors are unlikely to be the key determining variable. Conversely team dynamics and team psychology are vital to success in a closely-fought contest.

At **all** times an effective approach towards individual and team psychology will make the experience of team racing far more enjoyable to those participating, coaching, organising or officiating.

Being a member of a team gives a person the opportunity to experience high quality interaction with others, and to benefit from it. The factors which make being a team member different from other kinds of human interaction are not difficult to understand. Three factors can be highlighted as crucial:

1. **Goals** – In teams the members have a common goal and are committed to achieving it.
2. **Roles** – Each team member knows what they have agreed to do. Role definition can make things easier for coaches, helpers and team members.
3. **Communication** – Goals and roles need to be negotiated through a communication process. This communication needs to be open, honest and frequent.

8.1.3 Winning the battle of the minds

The psychological approach seems to be particularly important in team racing compared to other types of sailing. At a top level I think it becomes a major variable in determining which team wins. My theory to explain this is that the team racer has to make very **fast decisions** whilst at the same time applying **good spatial judgement** to complex situations.

In essence you need to have a clear mind so you can **act intuitively** and perform mental tasks like thought prioritisation without difficulty.

Of my four World Championship campaigns with **GBR1** the three times we won medals some focus was given to 'sports psychology' whilst the team was developing. This has been more necessary when a squad was used as the base for a team. It is important to **'know yourself'** so that this sort of training offers no particular threat to you. It is **normal** in all sport as part of preparation. A suitable coach or sports psychologist can facilitate sessions on communication and 'what if' analysis. This will help to build a robust team able to play the 'inner game' as well as they need to.

The **'inner game'** refers to the **challenges you face within your own mind**. It takes place against such obstacles as lapses in concentration, nervousness, self-doubt and self-condemnation. The inner game is the mind overcoming any habit which might inhibit excellence in performance.

Why should things like anxiety, anger, depression and self-doubt manifest themselves in connection with sport? Psychologists propose that this is to do with our pattern of culture. We live in an achievement-orientated society, which can give rise to these thoughts. There is no particular logic in measuring your worth by how well you do in one specific competition. You and the world are more significant than that.

Here are some tips to help cope under this strain imposed on your competitive soul:

1. Remember you are what you are, and not how well you perform at any particular moment (see the footnote below).

2. How you perform in a team race event may be an indication of how well the team performed and how hard you tried but it does not define one's identity nor give you cause to consider yourself as something more or less than what you were before the event.

3. Allow yourself to express spontaneity by avoiding playing some heavy ulterior game involving your self-image.

4. If you are feeling excessively anxious try to deal with this by an established method. One effective way is to concentrate on your own pattern of breathing. This focus settles the mind and lets you get on with performing.

5. If something unexpected upsets or annoys you, try to deal with it by laughing about it.

6. Do not get obsessed by who or what team is being 'lucky' or 'unlucky'. 'Luck' is not a controllable factor. Focus at all times on things you can control.

7. As a team member you need to talk to the other team members to know enough about their inner selves so that you can help each other to optimise your performances and hence that of the team as a whole. Sometimes this will mean individuals modifying their behaviour for the good of the team. Friends sail well as a team. **The strength is the team**.

8. Be robust in yourself. Do not depend on others to strengthen you psychologically all the time. This would make you vulnerable to outside influence and is not a sustainable way of being at your best.

Winning is about overcoming obstacles to reach a goal. A healthy overriding philosophy for a team to have is that reaching the goal itself may not be as valuable as the experiences that can come in making a supreme effort to overcome the obstacles involved. **The process**

can be more rewarding than the victory itself.

Sometimes when sailing I have felt a strong, unwavering determination to compete very effectively. In a strange and paradoxical way winning at that point mattered less to me but I found myself making my greatest effort. This sensation of competing 'outside oneself' is referred to in many descriptions of successful sporting moments. There is a **clarity and focus in the mind** and finding this state can be made to be almost routine if you train yourself to do it and make the effort. In this context you are your own coach but a good crew/helm partnership will understand each other's thinking and this can help a lot. Many crews I have sailed with have used certain key words to help get my thinking back on track if I am faltering. For example, I remember when I had just been given a second penalty turn at the Wilson Trophy. I was pretty annoyed and distracted. Mel Hughes said to me

it's not over …just sail

That was code for 'get on with what you do'.

Tip: You need to discover the game that you think is really worth playing

Footnote: Read Jonathan Livingston Seagull

8.1.4 Selection

A team selection process is easy to write about but can be very difficult in practice. There are a number of compromises to be made and much preparatory work to do before a final team is confirmed for the big event, and even then injury or outside circumstances may force a late replacement. You may even find that the issue is more one of team 'recruitment' in which case you can skip this section!

A team selection policy should take account of the key aims of the team or club. These may include restrictions (some possibly unfair) regarding age, sex or other eligibility factors. There may be a compromise between availability **versus** ability. It is easy to state that the selection is 'merit based' but team racing skills and team compatibility can be hard to assess. In the absence of an agreed selector I recommend that a team captain is nominated (helm or crew) and they take ultimate responsibility for selection following a thorough period of consultation with advisors and team members. The time scale available will determine whether one-off selection is going to be used or whether a team evolution process can occur as options are tried out. There is merit in sorting out team selection early on to allow time for the team to gel… but in competitive sport a place in a team is never guaranteed.

❏   Is there a compensatory place on a second team?
❏   Do you want to put together two or more balanced teams to promote local sailing?
❏   Is the team going to remain fixed for a length of time or is it dynamic?
❏   Will helms and crews be selected separately or as partnerships?

There is considerable merit in being seen to be fair. If selection decisions are very marginal then a form of trials, perhaps involving match racing or random two boat racing may provide some indicator. As a selector make sure that you have the respect of the people involved and clearly communicate your roles and goals and how these are driven by those of the group as a whole. Selection will inevitably be based on subjective assessment, however it is possible to build some logic into the decision process.

A selector should assess each sailor's team racing ability in terms of:

❏   team race skill
❏   speed
❏   rules knowledge and application
❏   ability to cope under pressure and fit in with the team.

Different sailors can be scored for these variables and the results discussed with them. Doing this early on in the selection process can be very revealing and motivating if the communication is handled sensibly.

8.1.5 Coaching and leadership

> **Learning**
> ❏   View success as a process, not a status
> ❏   Training is something that is done to you, but learning is something you take responsibility for

The role of the coach or leader is to promote high performance in:

❏   **task achievement**
❏   **team growth**
❏   **individual development**

In order to get these three to interact in the most appropriate way any coach needs to appreciate that there is a huge overlap between them and the skill will be to juggle and balance.

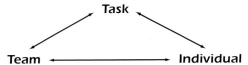

Due to the size and complexity of the overall task it is better for the leader to bear in mind that their fundamental role is to give direction and purpose to facilitate progress, not to issue directives.

❏   **All** the team or squad members should "know where **they** are going"

To achieve this state of affairs the coach (or team member–coach) needs to avoid the old fashioned 'preaching and telling' approach. It has been proved that these methods turn off the human mind. It literally shuts down and operates at a base level of attentiveness. People can only learn when the level of awareness is raised above the norm.

> **Awareness can be raised by:**
> ❏   avoiding telling people something they already know
> ❏   avoiding telling people "your" way of doing it
> ❏   avoiding implying it was "all" wrong
>
> **but instead concentrating on:**
> ❏   gathering high quality and relevant input
> ❏   encouraging people to be responsible for tasks
> ❏   saying what they need to hear and not what you want to say
> ❏   questioning the team/individual about the issue
> ❏   rating specifics (e.g., tacking quality, starting consistency)
>
> Under the high awareness conditions the solutions can be drawn out of the team or individual and it will be much more sustainable for having come from that route
>
> **Tip:**
> **As a coach you should admit your errors**

8.1.6 Practice options

As you have seen earlier on there are a number of important skills. It is important to realise that these cannot always be developed during a competition and that practice has an important role to play. Practice gives you a chance to try new techniques and make mistakes without repercussion. In order to have an effective practice it is important to consider the needs of all the team as well as the facilities and number of boats available.

The table below shows the type of practice which can occur with a given number of boats.

In '3 vs 2' racing you can use the last boat loses option. Alternatively one team can carry a 'ghost' fourth placed boat.

In 'piggy' it is important that the last boat is brought through to first by the efforts of the lead boat in order to allow all the boats to practice the various skills. The previous lead boat is then sandwiched in second and is the new 'piggy-in-the-middle'.

Wilson Trophy 2000 – Starboard hand windward marks always end up with some close situations. Here Nº7 has a starboard situation with Nº12, but if she forces Nº12 to tack that will also cause problems for Nº8, her team mate. If Nº7 tacked at the mark and Nº12 was close then Nº7 might foul under Rule 18.3 **Tacking at a Mark**. What would you do?

Table of Practice Options		
Type of Practice	N° of Boats	Key Skills Developed
Individual	1	Boat handling Timing
Match Racing	2	Roll tacks & gybes Control zones Boatspeed
Piggy-in-the-Middle or 2 vs 1	3	Slowing Acceleration Rules application
Two Boat	4	All the above Starting skills Communication Whole races
3 vs 2	5	All the above
3 vs 3	6	All the above
If extra people		Umpiring skills as well

If during practice the fleet gets too spread out, one or more boats can do a turn (or turns) or go to the back to bring the boats together. It is important to realise that it is a practice and to remember the goals you have agreed.

It is also interesting to practice doing just one leg from the perspective of a particular combination. Rather than wait for the combination scenario to happen in a practice race you can, instead, set up the combination deliberately. The boats line up on a reach in 'follow-my-leader' style and then proceed around the mark to commence the leg. You might choose to do this to practice tactics for managing the difficult combinations (e.g., 1st, 4th, 5th). It is important not to start racing until everyone is onto the leg. Review the learning points each time while sailing back to repeat the leg.

8.2 THE TEAM RACING RULES APPENDIX (ISAF Rules Appendix D) – An Explanation

Appendix D – Team Racing Rules carries a few modifications to the Racing Rules of Sailing. The modifications are intended to promote fair team racing with minimal need to be an expert on any specialist rules. None of the changes described need give the fleet or match racer any concern since they will have no difficulty with learning the modifications.

Appendix D of the Sailing Rules details rules that are specific to team racing or modifications to existing rules that are specific to team racing. This detail is useful for understanding the sport; this is because team racing has two main aims which underlie all the amendments to the standard rules. They are:

1. Team Racing should remain **as close to normal fleet racing as possible**. Rule modifications should be minimised and are only incorporated where absolutely needed to 'make the sport work'.
2. Team Racing should remain a 'self policing' sport as far as possible. This means that while the Team Racing Appendix gives provision for sailing with umpires and observers (referees) the sailors themselves should always carry the first burden of responsibility for keeping the rules.

8.2.1 The changes to the Rules
Rule 17.2 – Proper Course, Bearing Away
Team Racing Rule D1.1(a): on a downwind leg bearing away is **only** restricted when a boat has an opposition boat that is OVERLAPPED **to leeward**.
Fleet Racing Rule: if you are AHEAD or OVERLAPPED and within two lengths of another boat whilst on a downwind leg you cannot bear down on them.
Implication: In team racing **bearing down is a foul only when you are overlapped**. This has the effect of allowing a boat that is ahead to do more manoeuvring which may allow it to get in a position to attack the boat behind. Note that if the boat to leeward is on your team then it is OK to bear away towards them. It is important to note that the constraint on bearing down does not apply before the start when there is no proper course and it does not apply on a beat to windward. In those instances you can bear down on other boats as long as you respect the fact that you are give-way windward boat by keeping clear.

Rule 18.4 – Gybing at a mark
Team Racing Rule 1.1(b): Rule 18.4 is deleted in Team Racing.
Fleet Racing Rule: An inside boat at a gybe mark must gybe even if it is on opposite tacks (because under definitions the fact that they are near the mark makes them 'overlapped').
Implication: In team racing the ability to stop a race at a mark is an integral part of the sport. Therefore if you have **acquired luffing rights prior to a mark** you are allowed to sail on and take a boat away from the normal proper course to go round. This

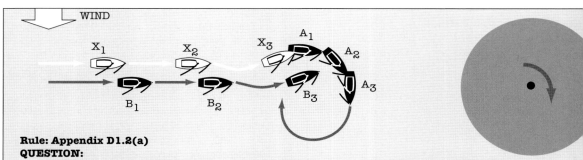

Rule: Appendix D1.2(a)
QUESTION:
A and B are "Team Mate Boats", A is ahead of both B and X and is taking a penalty turn. B luffs X
as they approach A. X protests – what should the call be?

ANSWER:
Green Flag – as long as there is no contact between them, team-mates can waive Rules of Part 2

Diagram 8.1: Waiving Rights of Way

includes a boat on starboard being able to luff up
to force a port-tack boat to gybe away from the
mark. As a normal interpretation you should have
acquired right of way on the inside prior to the
two length zone in order to have this power to
sail on and not go around the mark. Under
current interpretations you cannot acquire luffing
rights within the zone (for example, by gybing
twice) because the overlap is continuous (see the
Definitions). See Diagram 7.4.

Rule 22 – Interfering with another boat
Team Racing Rule D1.1 (c) & (d): These changes are
    additions to Rule 22, restricting a boat from
    interfering with another in certain circumstances.
Fleet Racing Rule: No rule – technically you can interfere
    with a boat on another leg when fleet racing.
Implication:
1. You cannot interfere with a boat **on another leg
    of the course**. You cannot be seen to hunt down
    an opponent but this does not prevent you from
    exerting right of way if your courses happen to
    cross.
    Note that if a boat has started prematurely it is
    considered to be on a different leg once it is
    returning to start. If a boat has finished it is
    considered to be on a different leg to one that
    has not. These clarifications of what constitutes
    'on a leg' are to avoid high risk manoeuvring
    very close to these already busy parts of a race,
    i.e., the start and the finish.
2. You must not actively interfere with a boat in
    another race. Any change of course you make
    which might affect a boat in another race has to
    be consistent with trying to compete in your own
    race. This prevents a person trying to influence

the results of a series of races by using a third
boat or a lucky opportunity to attack boats in
another race. I cannot recall ever seeing this
being done in recent times but I have seen races
lost because two races have got tangled up with
each other as boats fail to observe approaching
races. An advantage of the 'S' course or a box
course (see Diagram 1.5) is that they minimise the
chances of this happening because beating boats
are well separated from other legs.

Rule 41 – Outside Help
Team Racing Rule: Allows team-mates to help each other.
Implication: This is a frequently used option and allows
    a team mate to contribute valuable tactical advice
    or important information to team mates. It does not
    allow physical contact between boats or crews
    whilst racing nor would it extend to passing
    equipment between boats.

8.2.2 Modifications to Protests and Incident Management when team racing

There are some modifications to the way an incident
between team mates is treated in the rules. If the
incident involved a breach of Part 2 of the Rules (**when
boats meet**) then it is not relevant unless there was a
collision. This means **you can waive right-of-way to
a team mate boat**, even if in doing so your alteration
of course adversely affects an opposition boat that you
happen to have right of way over. For example, on a
reach a boat sees a team mate in front of her doing a
penalty turn. The boat is allowed to luff to avoid the
team mate and this is allowed to include luffing an
opposition boat at the same time. In Diagram 8.1 Black
B is allowed to luff to avoid A$_3$ even though waiving
rights like this has an adverse effect on White X.

There are a number of key points in the Appendix that aim to describe the team racing incident process. I detail a brief version of them below:

1. **When protesting a boat must fly a red flag.** In fleet racing this is no longer a requirement for small boats.

2. **A boat can exonerate itself by completing a 360° penalty turn** if it has committed a breach of the rules of Part 2 (when boats meet) or any modifications of those rules provided for in **Appendix D1 (Team Racing)**. A turn includes a tack and a gybe and completing a full circle.

3. If a boat is penalised or is taking a penalty turn on or near the finish it is not to be recorded as having finished until the penalty has been **completed** and it has **sailed completely on to the course side** before crossing to finish. Referring to point 2 above, a boat may start a turn above the line and loop around an end, but you would then have to tack to complete the turn before re-crossing the finish.

4. If one boat has completed a turn the protesting boat must stop displaying its red flag. You must also take the flag down if you change your mind and decide you were at fault after all and decide to do a turn yourself. Note that when a race is umpired the red flag is only displayed for a short time, usually by simply holding it in the air for 5–10 seconds.

5. It is possible in team racing to decide (using the sailing instructions) that **any protest can be held verbally** with no need for a written form to be completed.

The Appendix includes a description of the umpiring process. This is described elsewhere in the book.

You should especially note the strengthening of the powers of umpires to allow then to intervene when a boat commits **a breach of sportsmanship**. This, for example, means that if you hit a mark or another boat, or fail to complete a penalty turn correctly, **the Umpire may INITIATE** a penalty against you. This penalty could be extra turns or a protest hearing possibly resulting in extra points. This is quite a considerable change of emphasis from the pre-2001 Rules.

8.2.3 Modifications to scoring while team racing

The Appendix refines the scoring procedure with some important details:

1. Any boats finishing a race score points equal to their place. If you fail to finish or fail to race you are given the number of points of the boats entitled to race.

2. Scores can be increased by **10 points** when a boat has **caused damage** and broken Rule 14 (Damage) or she was **a premature starter** that did not return correctly. This means you cannot win unless someone in the other team also gets additional points.

3. If a boat has broken any other rule, but a penalty has not been taken, her score will be increased by 6 points. This means that in a three boat team race you could have a 1st, 2nd & 4th and still win; however I believe that if you did this knowingly you would have been unsporting and therefore subject to additional points (see above and point 4 below).

4. In addition a protest committee may further increase a team's score if one of them has broken a rule and they believe that their team **has gained an advantage as a result**.

5. The team with the lowest score wins. If there is a tie on points the combination of race scores that does **not** include first place wins. This is a critical modification that makes two versus two and four versus four team racing very exciting because key combinations like 1st, 2nd, 7th, 8th in four boat team racing is still a losing combination.

8.2.4 Other modifications to look for

The Appendix includes details on how to score a **series**. In the event of a tie on points in a series or league there is a clear tie break procedure. It is essential that this is referred to in the event of a tie so that the correct procedures are used. It includes details of how to handle part-completed series.

The Appendix concludes with a section on breakdowns when the organisers have supplied the boats (these are often modified by the Sailing Instructions). If you break down in a 'supplied' boat:

1. Fly a red flag.

2. Try to continue racing.

3. Try to obtain redress for the race to be resailed or for you to be awarded a fair position. If there is doubt as to the relevance of the breakdown do not expect much charity. The means by which the breakdown occurred is central to the decision reached and any carelessness on the part of the crew will count against it.

8.2.5 The relevance of the Sailing Instructions

In addition to the Appendix you also have to absorb the information included in the Sailing Instructions with which you are supplied. Some specific things to look out for are:

1. The recall procedures in use – specifically, what

signals and hails will be made when a boat or boats are On Course Side.

2. The type of marks and whether the flag (if marks carry them) is part of the mark.

3. The rule when capsizing because if the 'mast head rule' is in operation a capsized boat will be required to retire from a race. This is done in the interests of safety and to facilitate the race programme continuing with minimal interruption.

8.3 THE WINNING STRATEGY

8.3.1 Risk based decisions

By being observant and concentrating you will be able to spot changes in and around the racecourse. The changes might be subtle windshifts or obvious man-oeuvres by your opponents. If the change is small and you are already winning you have time to digest the situation, assess any opportunities and consider what the scope is for changing something easily. On the other hand, you might be losing badly, be near the end of the race and running out of options. There is a spectrum of manoeuvre options which will exist, at one end are very low risk options like making no manoeuvre or just loose covering, at the other end are aggressive mark traps and dynamic boat-on-boat tactics. Super-imposed on this is your view of how well you can perform in terms of skill which will also affect your choice of action.

If you have all the options and inputs then you are also able to decide how big a risk is necessary. The scenario may require a high risk manoeuvre option or perhaps a low risk option is best:

Table of Risk Options

LOW Risk choice BEST:	HIGHER Risk option may be BEST:
Currently winning	Currently losing
Long time remaining	Short time remaining
Shifty conditions	Steady breeze
Gusty conditions	Steady breeze
Your team is fast	Opposition is fast

Having mentally set out your table of risk options, combined with the inputs, you are in decision mode and can REVIEW what to do.

The problem is that, by now it's all happened… this is taking too long!! **Anticipation simplifies and speeds up the decision process.**

The good team racer looks at a situation and through experience and judgement decides what will happen if a particular action is taken. The sailor does this for all the boats racing that might affect him, but focuses on the events most relevant to his boat.

The helm thinks, (see Diagram 8.2)
"If he was to tack on to starboard I would…
- ❏ tack straight on top of him?
- ❏ tack into a loose cover?
- ❏ sail on and try and get across their other boat, he is much closer now since the shift?

It is really important for our team position that I catch that other boat since he is in second place and they have a 1st, 2nd combination. I think I am going to cross him. If the boat behind tacks underneath me I won't cover him, I'm going to try and get second."

Crew says "He's tacking off underneath"
Helm, **"We're carrying on"**

By the time it came to the decision moment, the helm was already prepared. This might seem like a very wasteful use of your brain time and effort, but it is a very powerful tool. Thinking ahead in this way will be the key to responding quicker. Faster reactions gain the advantage.

UK squad coaches advocate the 'two minute bubble' theory. This supposes that you can either choose to think about the two minutes that have just gone or you can look forward and anticipate what is going to happen and do something to change it. The brain has a natural tendency to reflect on the past. You must train yourself to look forward and use your 'two minute bubble' as a productive anticipation tool.

Top Tips for scanning the race course:
- ❏ The helm should advise the crew of particular boats that are of interest which need to be monitored
- ❏ The crew should monitor situations and inform the helm of critical moments such as after boats have completed a tack or when another boat gains or loses
- ❏ Communication from crew to helm should initially focus on the nearest enemy boats that threaten you. Describe …how far away? …who? …what tack?

Don't assume your team mates have spotted a new development in the race – Communicate

8.3.2 Managing the combinations

The strong team will identify the combination the boats are in and then ask the following questions:
- Who is winning?
- How stable is the combination?
- Which boats need to go fast?
- Which boats need to go slowly?

One coach pointed out that there is an even simpler way of reminding yourself of what really matters. He summarises this using the well known London Underground phrase of "Mind the Gap"! Essentially this means you should identify where in the combination is there a critical gap? Do you, as a team, want to attack the gap by closing up or overtaking, or do you need to defend the gap by opening out or maintaining the positions? Once you have decided where the gap is and what you need to achieve, you will automatically know whether to compress or slow, and whether or not you yourself are near the critical focus of the race. Diagram 1.12 shows how to protect your most vulnerable boat (the boat that needs to go fast) by double tacking at the leeward mark.

If your boat is some way away from the gap you should still be conscious of your indirect effect on the gap. At certain points in a race, the boats are almost like railway carriages in that the lead boat's speed will have a direct impact on the speed of all the boats that are behind it. This is true as boats slow on a reach, as they close up to one another and try to avoid overlaps; it is also true at marks when boats slow given their reluctance to go around the outside and the fact that they are not permitted to barge through on the inside. This virtual linkage of the boats is something that lead boats should be sensitive to. While stopping to compress the fleet is often a desirable manoeuvre, there is also a right moment to start accelerating again so as to minimise the chances of making life difficult for your team mates (see Diagram 1.13).

8.3.3 Managing 4-boat team racing combinations

In Part 1, I stated that the fundamental rule for 4-boat team racing was to score 18 points or less. If the scores are level then the rules state that the team with first place loses. Sometimes 4-boat sailing instructions change the scoring so that 8th place scores 8.25 points. This changes a couple of the combinations. Specifically, when 8th place scores 8.25 points:
- 1st, 4th, 6th, 7th – now wins, but
- 2nd, 3rd, 5th, 8th – now loses

It is useful to remember the following tactical/score guides:

1. **Get three boats in the top four and you win.**
   This is the most effective way of approaching the

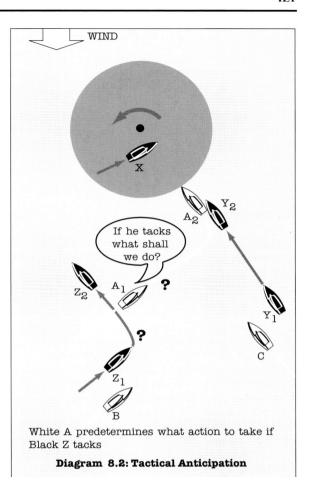

If he tacks what shall we do?

White A predetermines what action to take if Black Z tacks

Diagram 8.2: Tactical Anticipation

race and puts a great deal of importance on the third placed boat in your team. Look after this boat and it should avoid getting involved with the opposition in order to keep fourth or third place.

2. **Get 3rd, 4th, 5th, 6th and you win.**
   This combination effectively maroons the opposition at either end of the race and makes it very difficult for them. If in this combination keep trying to stretch the race to strengthen your position. Conversely if you find yourselves in 1st, 2nd and then **not** 3rd, you need to react very quickly to bring your 3rd/4th boats through otherwise you may be forced into this difficult combination. If you are stuck in 1st, 2nd, 7th, 8th, you need to try to compress the race and create incidents.

3. **Get an unstable winning combination and hold it**.
   This is difficult and liable to change. In order to make the maths easy remember that if you have a winning three boat combination (e.g., 2nd, 3rd, 5th)

in the top six and **not** 8th, then you are certainly winning. Remember also to be aware of which scoring system is in use and see the combinations it affects.

Basically you cannot go far wrong with your tactics if you keep trying to convert the combination for a better one until you can do no more. First is inherently less valuable (as in two boat), and anyone who says that 4-boat 'isn't really team racing' can't have sailed in or seen a close unstable race when all hell breaks lose as all the boats get tied up with each other. Enjoy!

8.4 UMPIRES AND INCIDENTS

The best way to gain an understanding of umpiring is to try having a go at it. Try this in practice and you will realise the difficulties involved. The key lesson is that you cannot expect umpires always to be right and you should not require them to be telepathic. So…

❏   **Communicate clearly,** and
❏   **Make genuine calls for an umpire's decision**

If you are confused with why a call was made in a particular way discuss the incident with the relevant umpire either between races or afterwards. If the call is something you still disagree with, **just get on with racing** and **do your turns**.

> **Top Tip:**
> In an incident ask yourself:
> ❏   Who had right of way?
> ❏   What additional obligations existed?
> ❏   How clear were the transitions?
> ❏   On balance were the answers in my favour?

8.4.1 Tips for Team Race Umpires

1.   Brief the competitors in a friendly and informative way. Be available for questions before, during (when practical), and after racing.
2.   Agree who is umpiring each race and try not to be a constraint on the program of races.
3.   Agree a system of assigning responsibility (to boats or areas) and agree a method for communicating between umpires (hand signals and/or radios).
4.   Control the boat. If you are accidentally getting in the way stop the boat and indicate you are an obstruction by shouting and by holding your arms out. Safety first, keep the speed down when near boats. Hang back a bit before the start and get closer to the action thereafter.
5.   If you are not able to be sure on a call use the green flag.

6.   Use a commentary method (describe what you see) to keep track of the action.
7.   If in doubt, go back to the point you were last sure of.
8.   Try to offer explanations at the time or after racing. Offer help… What could the sailor have done differently?
9.   Get a **Waterproof Notebook** (Fernhurst publish one) to record interesting or contentious calls for later.
10. Umpiring is difficult. Do some practice and this will help you and the team(s) that you work with. Encourage competitors to come out in the umpires' boat to see the other side of events.
11. Admit that you do not always get it right and be prepared to say as much to competitors.
12. Be tactful when feelings may well be running high – This is the way that I/we saw it…, for example.

Lastly, enjoy yourself and help to develop the sport by encouraging participation – Keep Smiling.

8.5 TEAM RACE CREWING

Team Race crewing is a **dynamic**, **exciting** and **skillful** part of the sport. The boat will be tacking and gybing more frequently than in fleet racing placing a bigger emphasis on the ability of the crew. The normal method used is to roll the boat during these manoeuvres so that the turn is assisted and the speed is maintained, this requires some slick and co-ordinated crew movements and these are the most skillful part of crewing the boat. In top-level competition the difference between teams may well be the difference in the ability of the crews.

In the winning team the crews will all be top level sailors many of whom will helm in fleet racing but choose to specialise in crewing when team racing. They will have formed **close working partnerships** with particular helms in order to optimise their sailing together. The partnership should be close to the optimum weight for sailing the boat.

The crew is much more than the person who trims the jib. They are the momentum behind the manoeuvres, the eyes and ears of the helm as well as confidante, coach, odd job man, diffuser, best mate and number one ally. They are the person the helm would be lost without. To be a good crew it is important to understand the separate requirements of each of these roles.

The requirements can be broken down into three main areas:
❏   **Boat handling**
❏   **Race handling**
❏   **Psychology - on and off the water**

Whilst all helms have slightly different quirks I believe that any helm would be happy with a crew who applied the following guidelines.

8.5.1 Crew boat handling:

1. Train to be agile and light footed and fit.
2. Wear high grip footwear.
3. Take the slack out of unused ('lazy') sheets and know where they are so that there is no delay when you start to tack or gybe.
4. Keep your weight well forward. To assist this in some boats it can pay to face aft when sailing in order to get your backside farther forward and so that you are more easily able to cross past the kicking strap (vang).
5. Make sure your hiking straps are the correct length for you (if you are allowed to adjust them).
6. Most inexperienced crews move too early and too gently in manoeuvres. Try to experiment by moving later and asking the helm 'how did that feel?'

8.5.2 Crew race handling:

1. If you are roll gybing make sure you get the plate well down so that the roll is controlled and smoothed out.
2. Be prepared to help sort out control of the kicker and mainsheet in the event that the helm needs assistance with any of these.
3. Try to keep the boat as tidy as possible. This includes masking any protruding cleats so they cannot catch on sheets, bailing and/or sponging the boat out, checking for any faults or equipment that is not functioning correctly. Your helm can help with these jobs as well, but they are initially your responsibility.
4. If the helm says 'PROTEST!' you fly a red flag clearly so the opposition and the umpire can see it. If the helm says 'UMPIRE!' you fly a yellow flag, again clearly visible. Make sure you have these flags available attached to some elastic and then on to you or the boat.
5. Try to keep your eyes out of the boat as much as possible to spot incoming boats.

8.5.3 Crew–Helm psychology:

1. Know what race number you are in next, when it is meant to start and who the opposition will be. Plastic envelopes and/or waterproof paper can be useful for storing this information.
2. Know what is happening with the other boats on your team. Check they are ready.
3. Know the course, many races have been lost because teams have sailed to the wrong mark.

4. If your helm is over-excited use your communication skills to calm them down so they sail at their best.
5. If your helm is half-asleep wake them up well before you have to go out to race.
6. Communicate the position of other boats and tactical information but be careful to do this in a simple way so that the helm does not get confused and over-loaded.
7. BE ENTHUSIASTIC
8. Watch other crews and partnerships for tips on handling and movement.

Great crews = great sailing partnerships

Great sailing partnerships = great sailing teams

Great sailing teams = Great Trophies!!!

8.5.4 Minimum Weight Limit

Note that in the World Championships a 130 kg minimum weight limit applies. I recommend this or a higher weight limit is applied by organisers to as many events as possible because it gets the sport away from having to have very light sailors in order to perform well in light weight dinghies. Clearly the International Sailing Federation agrees with this view. On a practical point the recent World Championships in the Czech Republic was the first to use the weight equalisation system and this incorporated the use of plastic containers filled up to the required weight with metal filings. In addition calibrated scales were at all times available to competitors.

8.6 TEAM RACING FOR KIDS

I have participated in the UK Optimist team racing Championship (as an umpire!) for a few years and have some observations developed from that and from discussions with people who have coached children extensively. **This section includes some ideas on possible ways to introduce everybody, not just children to the sport.**

There is no doubt that t**eaching team racing is a very worthwhile and rewarding experience**. If the racing is well matched the participants love it, all are involved, the battle between 5th and 6th is as important as that between 1st and 2nd. This enjoyment is especially true if there is a coach/umpire on hand to guide on rules and tactics.

There are several key skills to focus on:
1. The importance of the **right-of-way rules**. Beginners naturally do not want to have

collisions, as they are nervous as to the consequences. Children have been successfully taught the Rules by using this instinct as the key. Why do we have rules? Get them to answer that question (to avoid collisions and injuries) and they can soon see the need to have 'rules'. Over time the level of understanding will improve. Encourage some discussion off the water but keep it interesting and short. Use visual aids such as magnetic boats and diagrams to aid understanding. (See the note below)

Tips for starting to teach the Rules to kids:
1. **Windward** versus **Leeward** – You sit on the windward side of the boat and your body sticks over the side so you could be hurt if you hit another boat. When you sail you look toward the sails a lot of the time. This logic leads to the rule and it also means you should be careful when turning to windward so that other boats have time to respond.
2. **Clear astern** – The rudder is at the back of the boat and is used to control the boat. What happens if you hit it? Also when sailing you more often look where you are going not behind you.
3. **Port** versus **Starboard** – Somebody has to give way otherwise it would be a mess.

2. The importance of **controlling the speed of the boat**. To perform many of the team racing manoeuvres successfully the team racer needs to slow down or speed up. It is important to be able to handle the boat comfortably at all speeds, and to accelerate or decelerate effectively. These skills can be developed using follow-my-leader type exercises where the lead boat (or coach boat) is continually altering course and speed. After a few hours the main skills are developed but remember different winds equals different skills required.

3. **The ability to start**. This is the first skill which will be rewarded if it is performed well. If they get off the line first then they may not need to know points one and two. Training for basic starting technique needs to concentrate on time and distance judge-ment. There are many exercises for this most of which are covered in fleet race training. Practise makes perfect. Due to the enormous significance of the start a sailor who starts well can often be slow to pick up on the other points such as slowing and controlling other boats. This problem can be overcome by feeding boats into a training race in certain positions.

4. Lastly it is important to **foster a sense of team spirit** that is often lacking in normal sailing. This can become the key to kids really enjoying the sport. Encourage the teams to work together, initially by coming up with a team name but then following on to having a team plan, a team warm up and a team debrief which can be facilitated by a coach. Discussions should be very short and very positive. I have seen too many kids being criticised about their general sailing and team racing… this does not encourage them to try again. **If you cannot think of a positive remark, and preferably several, then say nothing!** Coaches and parents be warned!

8.6.1 Keep it simple…

Sometimes three boat team racing can be too complex for small children to understand, it is not always easy for them to know if they are winning or losing, or what they should concentrate on next. Two-boat team racing can be the answer. Two versus two with last boat loses is the definitive way to develop the understanding of the need for control and slowing down skills in combination with rules understanding.

As a guide to coaches it is important to appreciate some differences when you are helping those who are a bit younger.
1. You get cold more easily when you are smaller.
2. You need access to toilets and food just like an adult but possibly more frequently.
3. Youngsters do not like to concentrate for very long (ask a teacher) so training sessions should be broken up into short sections. Use fleet racing or time on the shore to do this.
4. Have a back up plan for bad weather, which can include food and games!

8.6.2 Safety

As with any sail training, in the current legal environment please ensure that appropriate safety precautions, insurance, equipment and people to use it are in place. If in doubt contact the national authority for advice. Generally team racing takes place on sheltered inland water so is at the low risk end of sailing options but do not be complacent.

8.6.3 Kids & the coach's mind-set

Before starting to coach team racing to children make sure you have your own aims and philosophy sorted out. **Your actions are critical for the future of the sport**. The main aim should be to develop a love of the sport, to impart into young children that training can be as much fun and as necessary as racing and that the skills learnt through team racing can be used to their advantage on the fleet racing course. **The fun should be what the kids see, the learning should be what they are doing**, and the philosophy should be something they just take on without ever realising it. Learning through play and experimentation.

8.7 WHAT IT'S ALL ABOUT... (REALLY)

The sport is so complex that people continue to develop their understanding of it for many years. There is no possibility of perfection. Enjoyment and improvement are the aims… along with bashing up the opposition in a true battle of body and mind!

8.8 BRINGING IT ALL TOGETHER

There is no doubt that one of the reasons team racing is so much fun is that it is a truly demanding activity. I hope you'll find you are able to give your thoughts on the subject some structure as a result of having read this book.

The task on the water allows insufficient time for detailed structured thinking. Instead you should remember that your objective is to train your mind so that the way you and your team mates think 'team racing' should become as automatic as possible. If you are confident and enjoying the sailing this is more likely to happen.

The complexities discussed in the book explain why, so often, experience can be seen to be important in team racing. This is true but I would also say that real talent and great teamwork can overcome many years of experience. Sharpness of mind and body can give an extra edge, a faster response and that winning advantage.

Do not expect to find team racing an easy sport to master. You cannot buy your way to the top. You cannot devote hours to solitary practice and expect to make a performance breakthrough.

Team Racing was designed to be enjoyable, socially rewarding as well as competitive, and to be approached in a spirit of good sportsmanship. If you take this attitude the pleasure of victory might be yours but the fulfiling rewards of participation in a fantastic team sport will certainly be with you. Ring your friends, find some boats, and get out there!

SOURCES OF INFORMATION & USEFUL ADDRESSES

Updates to this book can be found on the Fernhurst Books website:
www.fernhurstbooks.co.uk

Team Racing & all competitive sailing, is controlled by the Rules of the ISAF, many of which you will have already encountered in this book.
The ISAF also publish information on the Team Racing World Championships and the Rules
Their address is:
ISAF, Ocean Village,
Southampton, Hampshire, SO14 2AQ, UK
Website: **www.sailing.org**

Contact the **United Kingdom Team Racing Association (UKTRA)** for information on:
❏   Rules and Umpiring
❏   Race Management
❏   Funding and Resources
❏   Membership and Publicity
❏   Coaching
❏   The National Championships
❏   Development of the Sport – increasing participation

and specifically for:
❏   UKTRA Membership & Information
❏   The UK Team Racing Nationals & How to Enter…
❏   The UK Team Racing Squad & How to Apply…
❏   Coaching and Coaches for Team Racing in the UK…
   →   What facilities are there for coaching?
   →   Who coaches?
   →   And how do you get hold of them?
❏   Umpiring Team Racing…
   →   How to get hold of?
   →   How to become?

❏   UKTRA also publishes a series of booklets, such as:
   ■   Event Organisation and Management, by Geoff Jackson – really all you need to know on the subject
   ■   Current Team Racing Umpires' Calls Book
UKTRA, c/o RYA,
RYA House,
Eastleigh, Hampshire,
SO50 9YA, UK
Website: **www.teamracing.org**

The **United States Team Racing Association** can be contacted through:
www.ustra.org

The **British Universities Sailing Association (BUSA)**
BUSA,
c/o RYA,
RYA House,
Eastleigh, Hampshire,
SO50 9YA, UK
www.busa-gb.com

The **Firefly Class Association** provides information on the class schedule of team racing events. It also holds information on new and second hand boats. Their website is:
www.fireflysailing.co.uk

The UK **National Schools Sailing Association (NSSA)** can be reached through:
www.nssa.org.uk

The **British Schools Dinghy Racing Association (BSDRA)** can be reached at:
www.argonet.co.uk/arundelsch/bsdra.html

Of particular interest to **Team Racers** will be:

The Rules in Practice 2001–2004

[ISBN 1–898660–77–8]

Bryan Willis

The Rules in Practice 2001–2004 looks at the key situations that repeatedly occur on championship courses, from the viewpoint of each helmsman in turn, and summarises what each may, must, or cannot do. Armed with this information you will have the confidence to exploit your rights to the full both on the racecourse and in the protest room.

Bryan Willis chairs International Juries at major events throughout the world. He was chairman of the jury for the Sydney Olympics and Chairman and Chief Umpire at the America's Cup in 2000. He is currently a member of the ISAF Racing Rules Committee, on which he has served for over 20 years. He was chairman of the ISAF Race Management Committee and the ISAF Race Officials Committee, and was instrumental in the development of umpiring. **Bryan Willis** is also a Trustee of the **Eric Twiname Memorial Trust**

The Waterproof Notebook

[ISBN 1–898660–80–8]

An invaluable aid for all Team Racers out on the water

is the leading publisher of nautical books and publishes
a complete range of racing books

For a free, full-colour brochure listing all our books,
please write, phone, fax or e-mail us at:

**Fernhurst Books, Duke's Path, High Street,
Arundel, West Sussex, BN18 9AJ, UK**

Phone:	**01903 882277**
Fax:	**01903 882715**

e-mail: sales@fernhurstbooks.co.uk

Alternatively visit our Web site at:
http://**www.fernhurstbooks.co.uk**